ADVANCE PRAISE

"This is not the first work to seek to import Asian philosophies into business practice, nor is it the first to reflect on the relevance of the philosophies underpinning Japanese martial arts to business. It is, however, unique in two respects: it is written by an expatriate CEO who has succeeded spectacularly in flat and alien markets; and the martial art in question is Kyudo, a form of archery little known in the West. While the narratives of both themes make fascinating reading, their conjunction provides important lessons for practising managers, relating to balance, harmony, focus and perseverance. The key point is that strategic management has become twisted towards meeting measurable objectives as ends in themselves, rather than viewing them as signposts on the way to sustainable competitive advantage. The target should be the customer and the organisation should blend with the customer. This book is a major challenge to the kind of thinking which underpins the scorecard type of management and which has undermined true strategic management. Highly recommended."

J.R. Slater, Professor Emeritus,
Birmingham Business School

"Jérôme has found the business inspiration and guidance through Kyudo that the Japanese could not find on their own. We Japanese have a lot to learn from him."

Kengo Kuma, Architect and Professor,
University of Tokyo

"Global business success often requires not only logical and analytical skills, but a genuine understanding of the cultural and philosophical underpinnings of the society, politics, and economy in which one works. Jérôme Chouchan, a French businessman with extensive experience in Asia, has written an insightful book that applies the philosophy and spirit of the ancient martial art of Kyudo (the way of archery) to the world of business. This book will be of value to all those who aspire to attain impressive business results and 'hitting the target' through harmony with society, the group, and the self."

Glen S. Fukushima, former President, American Chamber of Commerce in Japan, former Deputy Assistant United States Trade Representative for Japan and China, former President and CEO, Airbus Japan

"In an era of intense and unpredictable change, both corporations and individuals need to maintain continuous attention and a firm, stable core. Jérôme Chouchan guides us along the path to achieving this in an inspiring and practical way."

Olavo Hartveld Cunha, Lead Officer, Patria Investimentos, former Managing Director, The Boston Consulting Group (BCG), Brazil

"Corporate Japan has been written about endlessly but Chouchan provides a unique insight on how the world can learn from traditional Japanese virtues. *Target* opens the window on a society that is still, in many senses, closed, providing the reader with an understanding of Japanese culture from the perspective of a long term resident who has garnered business accolades in Japan and across Asia. Chouchan attributes his success in commerce to mastering the ancient Japanese martial art of Kyudo and all it has taught the author about the modern day Japan in which he lives and works. This is a must read not only for those endeavouring to achieve commercial triumph in Japan, but anyone who has an interest or love for this fascinating and endearing country."

Michael Woodford MBE, former CEO,
Olympus Corporation and Whistleblower

"One of the many beautiful aspects of Japanese culture is the way it retains the threads of history through into modern life. None more so than the importance of how things are done, not just the outcome.

As western business and culture is now often about instant gratification, or the short-term result at any cost, little regard is given to the balance of how things are done. But for the Japanese, the way of doing things is conducted with high levels of respect, care and reverence, to the past, as much as to the future. While this is often frustrating to many 'non Japanese', it is a critical part of the way of life and of doing business in Japan.

Target deliberately and successfully links the discipline, care and reverence of Kyudo to that of conducting business. Seisha hitchū, 'Right shooting always results in a hit' gives a sense of focusing on why and how it will be done, ensuring a greater sense of accuracy and predictability. A must read for any leader living and working in Japan, as well as any business leader looking to build longevity and predictability within their business."

Mark Goddard, Group CEO, Hallenstein Glasson Holdings Limited, former President and Representative Director, Toys "R" Us Japan.

"I imagine Jérôme Chouchan, being French, had a hard time with understanding the nuance of the words spoken during the practice. In reading what he wrote here, I felt very refreshed, learning how he was thinking of and understanding Kyudo. Through practise, he understood that it is not just about aiming at a target, but it is a 'Way' to seek something much deeper. As a fellow archer, I am very happy to see his deep understanding of this. As a board Director of the International Kyudo Federation, he is doing a lot to popularize and promote Kyudo. As the thoughts and teachings of Kyudo spread, the world will become a better place. That is what I think, as someone who has been doing Kyudo for many years, and I do hope that will be the case. I hope more people will be interested in Kyudo through reading this book."

Takeo Ishikawa, President of International Kyudo Federation, Hanshi 9th dan

"Kyudo is a wonderful, traditional Japanese culture from ancient times. But compared to other martial arts, such as Judo and Kendo, many probably feel that Kyudo is not particularly well-known. Now, Jérôme Chouchan, a Frenchman, has written a book introducing Kyudo's way of thinking and its teachings and relevance from a business perspective; it will present a good opportunity to promote Kyudo to many people, as well as inspiring many to embody the valuable lessons Kyudo has to offer. Kyudo is a wonderful means by which to grow, through exercising the spirit and mind and seeking the truth, goodness, and beauty by aiming at the target. Jérôme Chouchan has introduced the vital lessons of Kyudo to the world through this book and explains how they have been transformative to both his personal life and his approach to business."

Takeshi Shibata, All Nippon Kyudo Federation, Hanshi 8th dan

Published by
LID Publishing Limited
The Record Hall, Studio 204,
16-16a Baldwins Gardens,
London EC1N 7RJ, UK

524 Broadway, 11th Floor, Suite 08-120,
New York, NY 10012, US

info@lidpublishing.com
www.lidpublishing.com

A member of:

BPR
Business Publishers Roundtable
www.businesspublishersroundtable.com

Printed in Great Britain by TJ International
ISBN: 978-1-911498-73-5

Cover and page design: Matthew Renaudin

JÉRÔME CHOUCHAN

TARGET

BUSINESS WISDOM FROM THE ANCIENT JAPANESE MARTIAL ART OF KYUDO

LONDON MONTERREY
MADRID SHANGHAI
MEXICO CITY BOGOTA
NEW YORK BUENOS AIRES
BARCELONA SAN FRANCISCO

CONTENTS

TO MASAKO, SANGAM AND NOÉ.

ACKNOWLEDGMENTS

Until I graduated from the business school HEC, I lived in France and, now, I have lived in Japan longer than that. I have learned many things from Japanese culture and Kyudo.

This book is the result of many encounters. I would like to express my special thanks to all of the people that I met.

I extend my deep appreciation to Hiroko Uragami, Hanshi, 10th dan, who has always watched over me; her daughter, Kaoru Kato, Kyoshi 6th dan; and everyone else at our dojo. I would like to also express my sincere gratitude to the Kyudo masters and members of the All Nippon Kyudo Federation, who have given me instruction, training, support, and helpful advice over the years.

I would like to thank William Reed, professor at the University of iCLA; Roger Pulvers, author; Philippe Grall, president of Equilibre; Richard Solomon, editor-in-chief of *Beacon Reports*; and Koji Chikitani of TranNet, all of whom gave me the encouragement to make this book a reality.

I am particularly grateful to my editor at LID Publishing, Sara Taheri, for her precious guidance on the manuscript. And I owe a special debt of gratitude to Tadashi Matsuoka and Keiko Takahashi, who worked with me on the Japanese version of the book.

Lastly, I would like to express my deep appreciation to Murat Ülker, chairman of Yildiz Holding, the parent company of Godiva, and to everyone at Godiva in Japan and worldwide, who gave me the inspiration for this book by enabling me to work in such a wonderful environment every day.

Thank you very much! Merci beaucoup!

JÉRÔME CHOUCHAN

INTRODUCTION

The secret to success in business lies in the principle: 'Right shooting always results in a hit.'

At first glance, archery and business seem to be worlds apart. However, surprisingly, learning the spirit and wisdom of traditional Japanese archery helps the modern businessman navigate through today's challenges.

Man is born with an irrepressible desire to hit the target he is aiming for. In archery, this means hitting your target with your arrow. Western archery has grown into a sport where accuracy is the sole measure of performance. Japanese archery, in contrast, has developed into a martial art where the spirit, the form and the accuracy all contribute to the criteria involved in assessing performance.

Born in France, in Paris, I visited Japan for the first time while I was exploring the world as a student at the French Business School, HEC. Later, I started to work in Tokyo and, 25 years later, I am still in Japan. I am currently the President of Godiva Japan, the leading premium chocolatier.

Godiva Japan doubled its revenue in just five years.

In this increasingly volatile age and considering a flat chocolate market, many have asked what type of business strategy and leadership have made it possible to achieve these results.

The answer didn't come from a business theory. It came from an unexpected inspiration that finds its source in the ancient Japanese martial art of Kyudo, which in English means 'the Way of the Bow'.

Kyudo is the traditional Japanese martial art of archery, which traces its origin back to the feudal period of Japan. Its spirit and practice have been influenced by the three spiritual currents, Zen, Shintoism, and Confucianism, which continue to have a profound influence upon the daily life and culture of the Japanese people to this day.

I have been practising Kyudo regularly for the past 25 years. From Monday to Friday, I routinely faced my business target: a budget with figures. At weekends, I faced my Kyudo target, which is made of paper and consists of black and white circles.

What is a target? The reason for its existence is to be hit. As an achiever, I have always pursued targets in my life. This ongoing desire is both exciting and frustrating, because there will be always hits and misses.

Kyudo contains a profound lesson that has been passed down from generation to generation: 'Right shooting always results in a hit.' This means that you do not need to worry or think about hitting your target. Instead you should focus your energy and willpower on a suitable mindset and form and, as a result of 'correct shooting' at the target, this approach will naturally result in a hit.

When this thinking is translated into a business context, the lesson is that if you sincerely care about the customers, and if the whole organization focuses its efforts towards customer happiness, then positive financial results will follow.

It may seem that this should go without saying but, on a practical level, you will find it difficult to put this thinking into practice as you fall under the pressure of sales targets, profit margins, efficiency and relationships in the workplace. In my case, I think the profound benefits of following the teachings of Kyudo have enabled me to unwaveringly follow through with this principle that 'right shooting always results in a hit'.

In the world of Kyudo, the correct approach entails a fight against yourself. It has nothing to do with your competitors or the circumstances you are in. The focus is simply upon you and the target, and everything is committed into your own hands. You are fully responsible for the outcome. I instinctively realized that in this thought lies the wisdom to establish and develop oneself, and the key to improving your relationship with others. That is why I started Kyudo. That is why I continue Kyudo, even when I feel moments of despair, at times when my shooting technique is not going as I wish.

Despite sensing a strong connection between the skills necessary to succeed in business and the wisdom that forms the heart of Kyudo, when I first started Kyudo I realized that there appeared to be an impenetrable barrier between global business and Japanese Kyudo. Global business is conventionally known for the pursuit of sales and profit, and often tainted by stories of greed and ego. In contrast, Kyudo is a traditional martial art governed by strict rules, and its core purpose is self-development and a pursuit of the perfection of the human being.

In Japan, business has been influenced by Western capitalism since the Meiji era (1868-1912) and has advanced remarkably through the Industrial and the Information Technology Revolutions. The business environment underwent dramatic changes in these times, whereas in the sphere of the traditional arts such as Kyudo (the Way of the Bow), Sado (the Way of Tea), and Kado (the Way of the Flower), the experience was different; in these areas, traditions have continued to be passed from masters to disciples for centuries without any changes.

In Japanese society, business and traditional culture are considered to be totally different worlds, with no integration between the two. However, being a foreigner, I was not bound by Japanese society's rules and established ideas, and this is probably why I was able to find some meaningful gateways between Kyudo and the business world.

Moreover, as I was pursuing a double career in business and Kyudo, I realized that the relationship between the target and the archer is similar to the relationship that exists between the customer and the company: the customer is the 'target', the company becomes the 'archer', the product is the 'arrow', and the resources act as the 'bow'.

In Kyudo, 'right shooting' means facing your inner self, performing your gestures according to the traditional rules of the art, and expressing this to the outside world. The same can be said of business. The work begins with facing yourself, performing actions according to the techniques of management and then expressing that to your business partners and customers. Once you learn to express yourself in your work, then you will find real meaning in what you do. As a result, the work will become more enjoyable and you will develop a much stronger sense of responsibility. You will get better results from each action and have more opportunities to reflect and grow as a person.

From an external perspective, it may seem that everything has been going very well for me. However, there have been times when I experienced inner conflicts between the values within me and those of the company, and, more generally, the outside world. At such times, I followed the teachings of Kyudo. Over time, Kyudo became a precious guide for my business. Applying the philosophy of Kyudo to business led me to new inspiration and discoveries, and taught me how to enjoy work despite the various adversities I encountered.

At this moment, you may be in the course of your career and feeling the way I felt before I encountered Kyudo: struggling with a gap between the reality of work and your ideals, and worrying about the future. Or you may be in a leadership position considering whether to implement a new company culture, where the purpose and the method of business actions is given the same importance as the company's financial results.

In this book, I will share some insights and solutions to the struggles and worries that anyone can fall prey to in their business and career. Even if you don't have direct knowledge or experience of Kyudo, you can still benefit from its universal teachings if you truly desire to improve yourself. What is important is to examine yourself each day and to continue endlessly to make an effort and strive to improve.

Kyudo is a word composed of two ideograms 'kyu' and do' and literally means 'the Way of the Bow'. 'Do' is a Japanese and Chinese ideogram that has two meanings: the literal meaning is a path that you travel; the spiritual meaning is Tao, the absolute principle of the universe, according to Chinese Taoist tradition.

Likewise, business can be pursued as a 'Way'. If you devote yourself to this Way of business and work hard, then you can develop and perfect your character while going through peaks and valleys, gaining joy and wisdom along the journey.

Godiva Japan currently accounts for around 40% of the total sales of the Godiva group. It became our number one market worldwide, both in sales and profit. However, from an outside perspective, this success presents a seemingly irreconcilable dichotomy: how could employees experience happiness in their work and the company increase its sales, without pressuring the staff with top-down orders to achieve those important targets?

I want to show that business can be both successful from a conventional standard of metrics, as well as spiritually meaningful when it is practised with a mindset that has a deeper goal than solely sales and profit. In this modern age, where there is a pressing need for meaning and fulfilment in the work place, the purpose of business should transcend simply mastering the techniques of management for the purpose of sales and profit.

Likewise, I have learned from Kyudo that shooting an arrow according to the Way can be much more rewarding and continually fulfilling for the heart and mind than simply learning how to pierce a target with an arrow. As a result, I believe that a Kyudo archer can be a symbol for the modern businessperson aiming at a target.

It is gratifying for me to know that readers of this book will gain insights that demonstrate a different way of approaching business.

PART 1

PRINCIPLES
FOR HITTING
YOUR TARGET

YOU DON'T REACH A TARGET... A TARGET REACHES YOU

Instead of aiming at the target, aim to become one with the target.

TARGET DISTANCE

"What's the secret to producing a hit?"

Whenever I am asked a question like this, I answer, "You don't reach a target; a target reaches you."

This is a saying in Kyudo. It teaches the importance of 'right shooting', which results in a natural hit, instead of constantly striving and aiming to hit the target. But this also raises a crucial question: how can we be in a state where we don't reach the target, but the target reaches us?

Well, that can be fundamentally difficult.

My interest in Kyudo was triggered by a book I read while I was studying business at HEC. It was titled *Zen in the Art of Archery* and was written by a German professor, Eugen Herrigel. In this book, Professor Herrigel described the Kyudo training he received while he was teaching at the Tohoku Imperial University in Japan. While he was teaching, he also wanted to learn about Zen, so he chose to study Kyudo.

His Kyudo teacher was Kenzo Awa, a Kyudo master and a man revered as a legend within the art of Kyudo. Herrigel quotes many of Awa's teachings. At first, I found many of his teachings bewildering, including the following:

"Throw the thought of hitting out of your mind! Let go of yourself, leave yourself and everything behind, so decisively that nothing more is left of you but a purposeless tension. Without letting oneself be put off by the target, stay at the highest tension until the shot falls from you. What stands in your way is that you have a much too wilful will. You think that what you do not do yourself does not happen."

What? Isn't Kyudo a sport where you're supposed to hit the target, with all your concentration on hitting?

This teaching seemed particularly baffling since Master Awa himself was so well known throughout Japan for his remarkable accuracy in shooting. How can you hit the target if you aren't wilfully aiming at it? Is it possible and efficient to throw away the thought of hitting, when *hitting* is what we desire the most at the moment of shooting?

Any beginner would have these questions about this teaching of Kyudo.

Since I was interested in Japanese culture and Zen, I thought I had at least some understanding of what these words meant. However, understanding with the mind and truly grasping a philosophy with the heart and body are two separate things. It was only after several years of following the practice of Kyudo that I began to truly understand the principle of 'not aiming at the target'.

Master Awa also says, "Don't aim at the target, instead the archer and target must become one."

For us beginners, 'not aiming at the target' in and of itself is paradoxical and hard to understand, but 'becoming one with the target' is totally beyond us. From the point of view of modern Western philosophy, influenced by the French philosopher Descartes, the subject and the object are clearly separated. It is therefore impossible to 'become one with the target'. In Eastern philosophy, this state of unity is beyond the mental, as the mental realm is one of dualism.

I was doubtful about these words in the beginning but, as I practiced Kyudo, I gradually understood the spirit and the philosophy behind the paradoxical statements.

One of the most important points in Kyudo is the distance between you and the target. Usually this is 28 meters and this great distance makes it very difficult to hit the target. When you stand in front of the target, you immediately feel this distance between yourself and the object you want to reach. The target looks impossibly small and you doubt that you could ever conceivably hit it. Since the distance takes you aback, you are overcome by voices of doubt in your mind and this pressure results in you missing the target.

Becoming one with the target is a process that involves allowing the distance – the distraction from shooting – to evaporate from your conscious mind. At the same time, it is important to allow your spirit and mind to lead your vital energy (ki) to expand endlessly in your whole body. If you are not conscious of the distance, then it becomes easier to hit the target. 'Becoming one with the target' is the ideal state for Kyudo. I am still far from having mastered this, and these moments of 'becoming one with the target' do not happen particularly frequently. Nevertheless, this ideal of unity provides me with a clear direction in my practice of Kyudo and also in business.

In the case of business, the 'target' is the customer in the market. The secret of business success is not reaching the target, but the target reaching you. Instead of aiming at the target, the customers, you let the target reach you, which then becomes a success. In order for this to happen, the feelings of the customer and the actions of the company have to become one. For example, if you place too much effort on advertising rather than focusing on the quality of the product, you are 'trying to reach the target'. However, this doesn't last long and will not truly succeed. When you become one with the feelings of the customer, the distance between the business, the product and the customer disappears, and success is achieved.

THE TARGET IS THE HEART OF THE CUSTOMER

When I was appointed as the president of Godiva Japan, I asked many friends what their impression of Godiva was. Their responses were straightforward. They acknowledged it as a premium chocolate brand, but when I asked them, "Have you bought it for yourself?" most of them replied, "I have received it as a gift, but never bought it for myself."

And they added, "It makes such a luxury impression that I am hesitant to enter the shop," or "The shop is far from where I live, so I only go there for special occasions."

After hearing these comments, I realized that the first thing to do was to make Godiva shops more accessible for the customer, and discussed this with colleagues soon after I joined the company. Some said, "Godiva is supposed to be an aspirational brand, much like a luxury brand of clothes and jewellery; a selective distribution should be maintained to create desirability." Others felt that, "We should extend consumer occasions and make it more accessible." Opinions were divided and a crucial question presented itself: are we luxury or mass? How can we accommodate these two seemingly conflicting thoughts?

In the workplace, where discussions are based on information such as statistics and graphs, logic and analysis of data prevail. But my practice of Kyudo has taught me that there is a realm beyond the dualism of the mind and we should endeavour to become one with the target. Going to the field is the business's way of solving the dilemma that lingers in the work place.

I visited one of the Godiva shops with my wife, posing as a customer. The Godiva shop had a premium appearance and was wonderfully luxurious. Simply looking at the beautiful and delicious chocolate increased our feelings of happiness. We instantly wished that there were more shops like this, more occasions to enjoy chocolates – in more accessible places. However, we were mindful of the fact that Godiva sells chocolate, not fancy items such as exclusive jewellery and clothing. Therefore we additionally felt that there was no need for the atmosphere to be too prestigious, which might seem imposing for potential customers, but rather it could be more vibrant and engaging.

At this time, my feelings had naturally become one with the target, the customer. In fact, I was becoming the consumer myself – feeling happy, forgetting that I was the president of a company that was fervently and eagerly trying to grow the business. Through this experience, I became convinced that Godiva could become simultaneously aspirational and accessible at the same time.

This is how our next strategic plan was created. Our hope was in the desire to transform Godiva into an aspirational brand that the customer would feel connected to in their hearts, but we also wanted the customer to find the brand accessible, so they would take the physical action of actually visiting a store. These two outcomes are not mutually exclusive and can be compatible.

As I explained these goals – and my experience in the store – to our employees, they all agreed. At first, they seemed to have conflicting opinions, but gradually they became unified behind a single vision for the brand.

GODIVA'S NEW STRATEGY

Now that our strategy was clear, we, the team of Godiva Japan, were able to establish three pillars as follows:

1. Advertising: strengthening the 'aspirational' visual factor by using television commercials with luxury codes.
2. Products: proposing the 'MY GODIVA' campaign to encourage people to treat themselves to Godiva chocolate, not simply to view it as a gift. This also involved the development of seasonal summer products such as ice cream, drinks and cookies.
3. Channels: exploring and developing new sales channels, including convenience stores. We also aimed to expand retail stores directly run by Godiva so that they could be found in all the 47 prefectures of Japan.

Overall, this strategy was a marvellous hit.

We had found our unique path (as shown in **Figure A** below). It was neither the luxury path, where an increase of point sales dilutes the brand image, nor the mass path where the development of point of sales is a barrier to building a premium image. This path was also different than what is called the 'masstige', or 'accessible luxury' segment because our price point is always the highest of the chocolate category in our distributor channels.

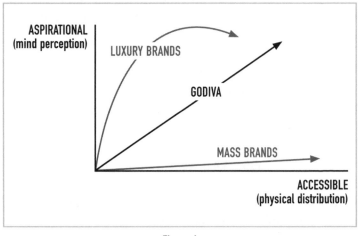

Figure A

All our retail channels experienced growth in sales, without cannibalizing each other. In Japan, no other brand, whatever the category, is distributed in such a multichannel environment. The reach of the product extends from prestigious department stores to accessible convenience stores. The chocolate market in Japan has grown by only 4% or so over the last 10 years, but Godiva has managed to double its growth within five years.

The Nikkei Research releases an annual Perception Quotient (PQ) summary report, "Store Strategy Survey," revealing the attractiveness ratings of 350 brands and stores.

The ratings are based on the perceptions of 240,000 general consumers. In 2017, Godiva was ranked fifth overall, within a list that consists mainly of everyday brands, such as 7-Eleven, IKEA, 100 yen shops etc. And in the sub category of, "I think the time spent there is premium", Godiva was ranked first in four consecutive years (2014, 2015, 2016 and 2017), above luxury brands such as Tiffany & Co., Louis Vuitton, Cartier, and Hermès.

It was a unique achievement to be the only brand ranked in the top 10 overall, as well as number one in the premium segment rankings. This gave substance to our goal, which was to make Godiva both aspirational and accessible.

The arrow that I shot had reached the target – the hearts of the customer. I personally visited one of the shops at that time and became one with the hearts of the customer, forgetting my own targets and role within the company. Becoming one with the customer was achieved through losing the distance between myself and the person who was buying the product. As in archery, when the arrow hits the target, this is a moment of truth from which a single insight is born. When it is true, this realization is without ego interference; it is beyond the logical mind. Such a singular insight – a sudden moment – has the potential to provide universal appeal to guide a new business strategy. Many successful startups or product innovations have been initiated when the CEO or founder became a genuine customer for their product or service, because they could not find it at a specific moment and then decided to create and launch the product or service. In his book, *Competing Against Luck*, Clayton Christensen describes the same phenomenon when explaining how the founder of Netflix began both as the CEO and as a target customer – there was no separation between the job of the innovator and the desire of the customer.

Instead of aiming at the target, we become one with the target: the customer. If the distance to the customer is removed, then you will hit the target without aiming for it. That is why this strategy touches the hearts of the customers. In business, it is important to think both as yourself and as the customer in the circumstance of purchasing and/or using the product or service. This is especially true if you are in a position of top management, where the distance between the customer and the company is the furthest. It is precisely by not aiming, therefore, that we accurately hit the target.

A PURE HEART AND MIND

2

Facing the target with a pure heart
and mind results in a hit.

LISTENING WITHOUT THINKING

In Zen, there is a word 'shinmuja.' This means 'pure thought'; thought that has not been tainted and one that is not evil. It describes a pure and honest heart, without desire. The calligraphy of shinmuja is displayed in the dojo (practise hall) of Nagoya. Dojo literally means the place (jo) to practice the Way (do). A dojo is revered as a special place and is very well cared for by its users.

Both within martial arts and in the tea ceremony there is a display of Japanese hanging scrolls with calligraphy from old Buddhist teachings, in order to inspire the practice of an intention that is spiritual in nature and which goes beyond the technical performance of the art. In shooting, we are taught to focus on correct shooting form and to shoot while preventing tainted or distracting thoughts from entering our minds. Distracting thoughts might consist of the following:

- 'I'll hit the target';
- 'I want to make myself look good to impress those who are watching';
- 'I might fail'.

These parasitic thoughts, born from the desire of the ego, are natural to everyone; they come and go during the shooting and it is only through practice that you gradually learn how to control and ignore them.

In business, it is also important to keep your heart pure if you are to produce a 'hit'. In the workplace, as in the archery practice hall, there are similar distracting thoughts that gravitate towards the focus of personal merit. We have all encountered situations in our career where we don't genuinely consider the feelings of the customers because we are trying to please our boss or colleagues, or hit our targets for professional or monetary gain.

We have all met executives who, first and foremost, plan their career advancement and always have in the back of their mind the thought, "What's in it for me?" Even if such executives have political skills that enable them to climb the career ladder, they are not the creators of a 'hit'. When such tainted and intrusive thoughts circulate in the organization, it prevents innovation.

The secret to producing a hit is for managers and employees to forget about themselves and face the customers with 'a pure heart'. It is a beneficial business practice to train oneself to listen to what customers have to say without thinking of personal gain and to tackle work with a selfless heart. Everyone takes pride in the way they do their work and the way they think; it is a natural urge. However, if your let your ideas take hold of you too soon, they become an obstacle to the vital task of listening to the feelings of the customers or understanding the opinions of those around you.

Those in management positions have a special wealth of experience. However, this experience can also become a negative force. It can cause a lack of flexibility, or a conservatism that can then make it very difficult to clearly hear what customers and subordinates are trying to say. The mind is always looking for patterns that it can reconcile with its experience and, even when the situation is new, it looks at it with old eyes. When the person in power is in this state, most often they are not aware of it and it becomes difficult for the subordinates to speak up; eventually the whole organization will fall into this same rigid state. Soon enough, the distance between the company and the customers will widen, making it difficult for the 'hit' phenomenon to occur. Whatsmore, the organization will lose agility and be unable to keep up with rapid changes in the market.

In the practice of Kyudo, the resistance power of the bow makes us think and feel that we need to deploy considerable strength to fully draw the bow. Naturally, every beginner will try to use all his willpower to draw the bow. Using so much strength results in an overly firm grip and stiff body, and therefore poor shooting.

My teacher told me, "You are fighting with the bow; you need to cooperate with the bow." He then quoted the tradition of the bow, which explains that real strength is born through the vital energy (ki) and the flexible use of the bones. Even 25 years later, though I have made some progress, I am still fighting with the bow. Each shot is different from the last, and I have learned through trial and error that the mind should be flexible enough to adapt to each new circumstance of the shooting. I discovered through this process that the mind is never as flexible as we would like it be.

Kyudo has taught me that flexibility is not a weakness but a source of strength. The top management of a company must be both strong and flexible. Leaders must make an effort to listen to both their subordinates and their customers by receiving input from them directly. I personally try to listen to people who are not involved in my business, particularly customers, by sincerely asking them, "What do you think about this brand, this product?" and continually to ask "why?" Understanding 'why' is the key to unlocking the vital experience of one unique customer; no quantitative data can capture this unique perception.

Questioning and listening is simple, and can reveal profound insights. As I ask people questions, I start understanding how the customers feel, and this gives me clues for products that may result in a major hit. Whether or not I can grasp them is dependent on the purity of my heart at that specific moment. As it is said in Zen, and then quoted by the late archery Master Uragami Sakae in his teaching scroll of the Heki Insai school, the mind should function as a clear mirror – a 'meikyo' – and it should reflect things as the moon does on still water – 'shi sui'.

THE BIRTH OF A BEST SELLER

Before my employment with Godiva Japan, I was a president of Lladro Japan. Lladro is a Spanish brand from Valencia dedicated to the creation of porcelain figurines. At that time, I had produced a big hit, a porcelain Hina doll for the Girls' Festival in March, and was involved in a project for creating a doll for the Boys' Festival in May. I was looking around at the dolls section in a department store, searching for some insights.

The sales clerk thought I was a customer and kindly explained to me about the dolls for the Boys' Festival. He told me the dolls for the Boys' Festival are displayed in Japanese houses on 5 May and are an expression of a wish that boys grow strong and healthy. Most of the displayed items represented samurai in armour, with a helmet and weapons, but we could not see the face of the samurai doll. I asked the sales staff how the young mothers perceived these dolls. He answered immediately that mothers perceived this style as impersonal and scary, and that they would have hoped for something more personal and relevant to their young children. This answer resonated in me because Lladro specializes in cute faces of children and women. In fact, that's what had captivated the hearts of people around the world since the company was created in 1953. In that precise moment, I realized that it would make enormous sense to redesign the Boys' Festival dolls with cute faces: this would respond to the desire of the target mother who was key to the purchase of the doll.

I decided that Lladro would sell Boys' Festival dolls. I was convinced that we should make their faces nice and gentle. I talked with one of the sculptors from the Head Office in Spain, and he showed special interest in the project. The challenge of making a cute boy's face that would appeal to the Japanese lit a fire in the young sculptor's heart. I resisted the temptation to give him instructions regarding what is 'cute' according to Japanese culture and trusted his own artistic sense.

A few months later, the Boys' Festival doll arrived. He looked cute; somewhat helpless and on the verge of crying. The sculptor had never been to Japan, but had created a boy's face so unique that it would appeal to a Japanese mother's instinct. What I received with a pure heart, he then received with a pure heart as well, and made it into something tangible.

When I saw the face of this doll, I was confident that it would succeed. All of the Lladro staff got behind it and sold them. Although the buyers from the department stores were not initially interested in a Japanese doll created by a foreigner, once they saw the doll's face, they went for it. That's how the Boys' Festival doll, which we named 'Wakamusha' (young warrior), became a big hit. One buyer from a department store told me, "This is the first time a foreign brand has been so successful in adapting something very Japanese."

I had sincerely listened to a shop clerk at the doll section of a department store with a pure heart, and I believe that it was this conversation that gave birth to Wakamusha.

The target is still, like calm water, and is always there. If you want to hit the target, you must first put aside your preconceived ideas and your own goals, and face your customers and your job with a pure heart. That is the beginning of a business that results in a hit.

Boys' Festival Doll, 'Wakamusha' by Lladro.

RIGHT SHOOTING ALWAYS RESULTS IN A HIT

3

Don't let your mind be captivated by your desired outcome: aim to get the entire process right and your business will succeed.

TRUE PURPOSE OF BUSINESS

I once asked one of the sales directors at Godiva, "What do you look at first when you go and visit a shop?"

She replied, "I check if the shop is nice and clean." Most sales people look at sales, profit, traffic, and conversion rate and then evaluate the shop based on those figures. However, she not only looked at the numbers, but also paid attention to how the products were being sold and the process of it all. And, as she had said, the shops that were clean – and therefore appealing – also had good sales performance.

As I listened to her, I remembered my Kyudo teacher had told me that, during exams, archers are observed by the judges from the moment they enter the Kyudo practice hall until they leave. This includes their posture and movement as they wait and walk, and how this is performed in a harmonious rhythm with other archers. The whole process is called 'taihai.' Taihai consists of the two kanji: 'tai', which literally means 'body form', and 'hai', which implies the notion of arranging and distributing the form. From looking at the taihai, judges get a strong sense of whether or not the archer will succeed in his shooting. They certainly don't make a judgment based simply on whether or not the arrow hits the target.

This brings us back to the important saying in Kyudo, that 'right shooting always results in a hit' (seicha hitchu). The kanji 'sei' 正 means literally 'right', 'straight' and 'correct', and has also the moral meanings of 'righteousness' and being 'truthful'. But what does it mean to shoot the arrow in the right way? Kyudo has a principle called 'shaho-hassetsu', which includes eight fundamental stages of shooting, from the placement of the feet until after the arrow has been shot. The eight stages of shooting 'sha-ho-hassetsu', as described in the Kyudo manual published by the All Nippon Kyudo Federation, are:

- 'Ashibumi' – placing of the feet. Both toes are placed in a straight line to the target. This is the first movement and the foundation of the shooting: the body posture should be straight.
- 'Dozukuri' – forming the torso. The spine and the neck are stretched, while the centre of gravity is placed in the abdominal region (in martial art tradition this is called 'hara' or 'tanden', and describes not only a physical point below the navel but also a centre of energy that radiates through the whole body).
- 'Yugamae' – readying the bow. This is the last preparatory stage before the actual shooting. The grip of the string is arranged with the right hand and the grip of the bow with the left hand. It is important to grip the bow and the string without too much strength, as this will influence the working of the bow and the flight of the arrow. Then the gaze is set calmly on the target, without thought of technically aiming.
- 'Uchiokoshi' – raising the bow. The bow is lifted with a peaceful feeling, like smoke calmly rising up on a windless day.
- 'Hikiwake' – drawing the bow. The bow is drawing apart equally to the left and the right, keeping the arrow horizontal during the whole movement. The drawing apart is not done only by the hands, but by using efficiently the whole body.
- 'Kai' – full draw. This is when the heart, mind, and vital energy (ki) should be harmonized as one with the bow and the arrow. This unity of mind and body is built on the cross of the body, made by the vertical axis of the spine, and the horizontal axis of the shoulders and arms. It is said that, during this stage, the spirit and vital energy should flow without stopping to the whole body and beyond, to 'heaven and earth', as well to the left and right, until the moment of releasing the arrow comes by itself.

- 'Hanare' – release. Hanare means to 'separate from'. It describes the moment when the arrow leaves the bow. The archer should not plan and think of the moment of hanare; it should happen as a natural outcome of the endless extension of the precedent stage of Kai. A good hanare will display sharpness and beauty. The body is firmly settled on his vertical axis, while the hands and arms unfold simultaneously along a straight line.
- 'Zanshin' – remaining spirit and body. After the arrow has left the bow, the shooting is not yet completed. The follow through action of the heart and body shows a dignified energy and form in continuity of the release. Whatever the outcome of the shooting, hit or miss, the archer does not express contentment or disappointment with his performance. With composure, the archer lowers his bow.

The shooting has been divided into these eight movements for the purpose of teaching, but all the movements are to be performed in a continuous flow, with each movement evolving naturally into the next movement. During each movement, you should focus your spirit, mind and body on doing the correct movement as you have been taught. You focus on the moment of each movement, and do not let your analytical mind wonder about the prior or next movement.

Kyudo teachers will check to see if you go through all of these movements correctly and will help you to constantly reach a higher technical level at each stage. Masters do the same eight movements as beginners, and the aim for both a master and a beginner is to improve shooting skills along the ideal of 'correct shooting'.

Although Kyudo is a sport of hitting the target, the masters never focus solely on teaching you how to hit the target. In training, the teacher never says, "You missed 50% of your targets. Why are you not hitting better?" Kyudo values the process of shooting, from beginning to end, rather than the result. The philosophy underpinning the art of Kyudo is all about placing value on the process, the correct spirit and form, not just upon the outcome. It is said in the Kyudo manual: "Our goal in Kyudo is not hitting the target. On the contrary, the expression of harmonious beauty is the objective of the shooting." The uniqueness of Kyudo is that your inner mental state is expressed in an objective form, through the body, bow, arrow, and target. The performance of the eight stages of shooting require a unity of spirit (kokoro) and technique (waza). The technique is expressed through the skilful use of the body and the bow. In his journey of the search of excellence in technique, the archer will simultaneously have to work on qualities of his character though discipline and self-control. These qualities are universal, and they are emphasized in the teachings of Confucius and Zen, such as sincerity (makoto), propriety (rei), benevolence (jin), courage (yu), and ordinary mind (heijo shin).

This focus on 'correct shooting' does not mean that hitting is not important. To evaluate your shooting progress along the journey, there are regular shooting tests, from the 1st grade (dan) to the to 8th grade, where archers perform in front of a jury of master archers. From the 4th dan and above, each of your two arrows must hit the target to be eligible for passing the examination. In addition to accuracy, the jury evaluates the level of the shooting according to the prescribed form that has been transmitted from generation to generation. On the journey to progress through higher grades, stricter attention is placed on the refinement of the movements, the dignity of the shooting, and the beauty and sharpness of the release.

Above the 8th dan, there are no more shooting examinations, but there are still two possible grades to be obtained: the 9th and 10th dan are awarded to archers who exemplify the highest level of conduct, dignity, discernment and ability.

In our everyday shooting, we try with sincerity to perform each shot to the utmost of our understanding and ability. The teaching that 'right shooting always results in a hit' is not only applied to each single shot by the archer, but also by the teacher during instruction. In my first years of learning Kyudo, when I was concerned about my poor accuracy at hitting the target and feeling impatient, my teacher used to say, "When you practice, just do your best to build the correct form with your body, and the regular hitting of the target will come in due time, naturally." Self-doubt about the result is replaced by the firm belief that if you do your best to perform the correct shooting techniques, the hit will be a natural consequence. When you place your feet on the shooting ground and face the target, you therefore chase from your mind all thoughts of success and failure, and focus your thoughts and vital energy on the correct posture and movements.

This thinking is very positive and helps you to gain inner peace, even when you know you have to deliver results. All we need to do is focus on executing each action properly, without being trapped by the emotional ups and downs when we are focused simply on the result. To be fixed on the thought of results is similar to what the Zen monk Takuan called "the delusion of the stopping mind" in his letter, *The Mysterious Record of Immovable Wisdom*, to the sword master Yagyu Munenori in the 17th century.

Having practiced Kyudo for more than 25 years, the way of 'correct shooting' has gradually permeated into my way of doing business. This has created a paradigm shift, from viewing first and foremost the top and bottom line of the business, to now first viewing the correct actions for consumers. However, this thinking is counter-intuitive in the corporate world. The management of listed companies, who face the pressure of achieving quarterly earnings, typically issue orders to achieve targets. In the course of my career, when I hit my targets, I often felt like a king. I also often encountered managers who continuously requested me to sell more, to achieve more. And when I missed my targets, they demanded, "Why have you missed your targets? Work harder and find new ways!" This left me with worries, low self-esteem and self-criticism. This cycle of instructions focused on the targets, coupled with the firing of poor performers, only succeeded in filling the organization with anxiety, self-doubt, and fear of failure. As a consequence, the employees felt disengaged, stressed, and undervalued.

In Japanese archery, hitting a target is a result of proper form, not a goal. In business, sales are the result of the actions of all the staff. It is a result of doing the right things, and it is not a purpose in itself. If you are focused solely on the result, then you will lose sight of the true purpose.

Godiva is a company that sells chocolate, but our core purpose is to bring moments of happiness to people throughout the world via chocolate. In order to accomplish this purpose, we need to create and sell high-quality delicious chocolate so that the customer will purchase our products happily and willingly. If we make that our top priority and get the process right, then the sales results and profits will come naturally. So, the female director that I mentioned earlier got it right – her way of thinking was the business version of 'right shooting always results in a hit'.

ENACTING SALES STEPS IN THE RIGHT WAY

Godiva Japan has over 288 shops throughout Japan. Each shop has its own sales goal. But these goals are achieved as a result of enacting the right sales steps, as in the teachings of Kyudo.

The in-store sales steps can be divided in the following way:

1. Adjust stock so that we can fulfil the requests of our customers at any time.
2. Make our shops accessible and easy to shop at.
3. Display our chocolates and gift boxes beautifully in the showcase at all times.
4. Keep the shops thoroughly clean so that our customers feel the appetite appeal of the products.
5. Improve customer service skills so that our customers can truly enjoy their time spent shopping.

I have placed importance on performing these five steps correctly, as I see them as the business version of the eight fundamental stages of shooting.

In order to implement these steps correctly, the cooperation of, and harmony among, all staff in each shop is essential. Our Japanese staff accepted this quite naturally, and implemented the Kyudo principles without a hitch. I was extremely impressed with that. The Japanese are highly skilled at following the correct steps required in order to take care of things. Perhaps then, the Kyudo mindset is an inborn skill of the Japanese people.

SETTING SALES AS YOUR GOALS WILL LEAD TO FAILURE

A good example that demonstrates how focusing too much on improving sales can result in failure is demonstrated by store operation.

In the past, some shops practised management based on the individual staff's sales performance. Doing this caused the staff to become overly concerned with sales results, and the operation of the shops suffered.

For example, when staff members were in charge of inventory management, they couldn't spend their time on sales, which kept them from receiving the incentive (bonus) that was given to those with good sales performance. This led to them neglecting to properly take care of inventory, as they wanted to boost their own personal sales results.

Managing staff on the basis of sales performance goes against the attitude of Kyudo. When the company's goal is sales performance, it places the burden on the employees and they can become demotivated, because increasing sales is not the true purpose of work.

In contrast, the principle of 'right shooting always results in a hit' encourages the employees to be creative, cheerful, and positive because they don't have to worry about their sales results, which can be very unstable for a variety of reasons. They are free of stress and can thus take more initiative at work. Instead of worrying about results, they are able to put their best effort into performing. This approach results in better engagement of employees. In a few years, our Godiva Japan business unit has moved from being average to being top within our global engagement survey.

Another good example in retail is Apple. Everything is organized around focusing the retail staff on giving the best possible consumer experience. There is no pressure on achieving sales targets. However, there are sophisticated performance indicators to track that the staff are giving the best service possible (including feedback surveys from consumers and feedback from colleagues). As one high-performing sales staff member at Apple explained, "This is very motivating for me because everything is about experience. Experience is completely under my control; sales are not. Metrics are here to track the experience, not the dollars."

The principle of 'right shooting' does not mean that this is a relaxing path. In striving to build the correct form in Kyudo, a tough level of discipline is required, which involves constant practice and effort. Essentially, this is because the mind and the body do not act as we wish. This discipline is called 'shugyo' – this is the same word that is used to describe the training of the monks in a monastery.

In Kyudo, as in business, you can always improve your form because you can always create a better product, use better advertising, and provide a better consumer experience. The role of a leader is to encourage everyone to do their best to improve the business and identify the metrics to work on, while not being under the tyranny of the sales numbers.

Godiva Japan doubled its sales in five years, over the period 2010-2015, by consistently achieving double-digit growth each year.

Personally, I never set a goal of doubling sales. Business heads from multinational headquarters experience pressure and often set very challenging targets as a result. Our thinking at Godiva was the opposite; due to the market conditions, our initial budget was set to increase by a few percent year after a year. However, our team put forth their best efforts, aiming to do the right thing every day, and thus was able to deliver double-digit growth year after year, performing strongly in the market. With these results, global colleagues began to wonder if we were elaborating our annual budget with a sandbag approach. In reality, we were simply following the principles of 'right shooting' to the utmost of our capacity.

Results will always follow when this mindset is used and if the entire process is done right. It is not only demotivating but also counterproductive to allow the mind to be captivated by the target.

By thinking in this way, you realize that the principle of 'right shooting' is an encouragement to do what you can do each moment with utmost care. Thinking about future results can make us nervous and/or worried and cause us to lose sight of the correct form and the journey. If we are to hit the target, it's important to do what we can in the right way, with care. But often we forget about this important principle because of the seduction of the target upon us. This is a universal truth that is applicable not only to Kyudo but also to life and business.

In Kyudo, as well as in business, I always aim to execute 'right shooting'. I believe that outcome follows form, in both kyudo as well as in management.

The same universal principle is expressed in verse 2, 47 of the 3rd century Hindu scripture *Bhagavad Gita*:

To action alone hast thou a right
and never at all to its fruits;
let not the fruits of action be thy motive;
neither let there be in thee any attachment to inaction.

This sacred verse always cheers me. The teaching of the *Bhagavad Gita* explains the way of action (karma yoga) as a spiritual journey when practiced with the correct intention. It teaches about selfless and desireless action (nishkama karma). In other words, we should not focus our actions on the reward of the target. This "desireless action" is different from a "desire for no action", which is only laziness and "attachment to inaction".

Therefore, focus on the right action as your duty, without worrying about the outcome.

RIGHT SHOOTING RESULTS IN A TRUE HIT

4

Make it your goal to shoot right. This is the key to long-lasting business.

THE 'RIGHT POSTURE' FOR BUSINESS

In the Kyudo examination, you can fail even if the arrow hits the target. Why is that so? This thinking is very different from Western archery, where a hit is a hit, without notions of true or false, and the arrow placement in the target gives you the same amount of points, regardless of how the shot has been performed.

'Right shooting results in a true hit' (seicha seichu) means that you have to face the target with a pure state of mind and correct posture, and then hit the target. But the arrow can hit the target accidentally without the archer being in the right state of mind or having the correct posture, which is why you can fail even if the arrow hits the target. In Japanese, the word posture is 'shisei'. But Shisei has a broader meaning than posture. Shisei describes not only an exterior appearance but also an interior intention and force, which is manifested in a visible shape.

Having the correct posture means to aim to express through your shooting the qualities of truth, goodness and beauty. These attributes are like the archetypes of Plato; they are intangibles, existent only in the world of ideas. Everyone can grasp their essences intellectually. The archer tries his best to manifest these qualities throughout the stages and journey of shooting. Those who look at the performance of a master archer can feel the expression of these ideal qualities.

In the Kyudo examination, form is judged according to the standard of the art of Kyudo. For example, at the moment of releasing the arrow, by looking at the movement of the hands and the body, the judges can see if the archer is in the proper state of mind and energy or if he has been overcome by the desire to hit the target.

The world of business can follow the same process. As Kyudo instructs us in the art of correct shooting (sei cha), we must think about what is 'correct' management in business. It is not only about external results, as the moral meaning of the character 'sei' implies. In the *Analects of Confucius*, leadership is explained with the same ideogram as right shooting ('cheng' in Chinese, 'sei' in Japanese 正): "To govern is to correct (cheng)." (Analects, 12:17) The example of Shibusawa Eiichi (1840-1931), a successful Japanese banker and entrepreneur in the Meiji period, known as the 'father of Japanese capitalism', shows that economic development and the search for righteousness can coexist. He continuously advocated what he called 'harmony between virtue and economy' (dotoku keizai goitsu), based on the philosophy on the Analects.

Companies that are only seeking profit can come upon a 'big hit' by chance. But, if things are then handled in the wrong way, the success is not sustainable, and eventually the market and society will not recognize or accept them.

So what constitutes the right posture in business? This seemingly elusive goal can be achieved by thinking about the customer, the employee, and by performing business tasks with a high morale.

Unless you go about your business with the right posture, your customers will not be truly fulfilled. Products and services have to hit the mark by satisfying the hearts of customers.

Are your products of good quality? Are they priced appropriately? Are they being sold in the right places? Is proper service being given? The top people of a company have to constantly ask themselves and their employees these questions.

If you aim to satisfy your customers through high quality, then your job will become enjoyable, as you are not just seeking a profit, but aiming for a higher, more meaningful purpose.

On the other hand, there are companies that value profit above all else and make decisions regarding the quality of the products, cost price, and sales price accordingly. When profits and sales are the only criteria for success, then all you think about are the figures and quantity becomes the guiding principle, at the expense of quality.

Some companies in Europe, America and Asia make a shift once they become public companies listed in the stock exchange: they transform from valuing the quality of their products and the benefits they offer to the consumer, to being primarily concerned about the stock market. Professionals who bolster stock market prices join the management team of the company; every quarter, they take measures to increase stock prices. They tend to yield to the forces of short-term gain. When management is overcome by the desire to hit financial targets, it enters a vicious spiral of always chasing higher numbers, which, in the worst case, may result in fraud. In the past, we have seen numerous cases of scandals from established companies, such as Enron, Goldman Sachs, Wells Fargo, Volkswagen, Kobe Steel and many others.

The root cause is that, in their desire to hit the target, the management has compromised the pursuit of the 'right' posture. This type of compromise can also be seen in everyday decisions, which at the time may seem inconsequential.

In one particular case, I remember the CEO of a manufacturer told me: "We try to reduce the cost as much as possible where it is not exposed to the eyes of the customers." But is this the right approach? The customer will feel that their trust was betrayed if the product looks wonderful on the surface, but the manufacturer is cutting corners behind the scenes. Once a company starts to value profit only, then the employees stop caring about the quality. The customers then sense this and switch to another company. Once that happens, it becomes very difficult to win the customer back. This type of management thinking creates serious issues for the company in the long run. As has been said in the Chinese classic book *I Ching*: "By walking on frost, ice will come."

Hitting the target is one of the outward proofs of proper shooting, but it is not a sufficient condition. In business, if sales and profit are badly missed, it indicates that something is not working within the company; on the other hand, if the numbers have been met, it does not automatically mean that everything is working properly.

THE LAW OF HARMONY

Profit is not the goal. Profit is the result of providing satisfaction to the customer; they are our target. The resulting profit then becomes a measure of whether all the departments of the company, such as R&D, manufacturing, IT, human resources, finance, sales and marketing, are doing their part and working in harmony. If you are not making a profit, then it means that there are problems or there is a misalignment somewhere. It could be, for example, that products are priced according to internal financial metrics, with a lack of attention paid to sales; or it might be that products have been manufactured by the engineers, ignoring the needs of marketing.

As mentioned earlier, correct shooting in Kyudo requires each part of the body to work in harmony in the eight stages of shooting the arrow. When the right and left arms, the chest, and back muscles each play their roles perfectly, shooting in harmony is realized. In order to shoot right, each part of the body needs to work in harmony with the rest. In practice, this is very difficult to embody because the mind works in only one direction, and often we find ourselves putting too much strength in the right arm or the left hand at the expense of other parts of the body. Through success and failures, we learn how each part of the body is influencing the others, and how it can impact the quality of shooting. The search for balance needs both analytical and intuitive working of the mind and body.

This law of harmony applies to companies. The operating profit of a company is the result of each department functioning effectively in harmony with proper balance while facing the target. As in shooting, there are always tensions in the body of the company and searching for balance and equilibrium is one of the continuous tasks of management.

The purpose of business is to contribute to society. The way to do this is through building sustainable and healthy growth. In today's business environment, keeping up with financial pressures, the pace of change, and globalization can be major challenges for shareholders, the leaders, and the employees. In these turbulent times, everything is moving around us so fast that we need a principle that is superior to these changes, one that can guide our actions.

The spirit of 'right shooting results in a true hit' is a solid principle to build, maintain and develop a company in this new business age.

the point that this natural moment happens. In the West, we have often misunderstood the principle of 'non-doing' with 'taking no action' and passivity, whereas in fact 'non-doing' is the fullness of action. It is action that is pure, without interference of ego and personal desire, so that spontaneity from nature (shizen) can happen. This is called 'doing without doing' (wei wu wei) in chapter 63 of *Tao Te Ching*.

MAKE IT SO THAT YOU DO NOT SELL YOUR PRODUCT, BUT IT 'SELLS' NATURALLY

We have to execute our best efforts up to that moment when the results of our actions happen spontaneously.

Similarly, we do not 'sell' products, rather, they 'get bought'. We have to do everything right, from the step when we conceive the product idea through to the step it is displayed and presented to the consumers. We keep doing our best until the moment comes when the consumer buys it by himself. This is the natural moment of sale. It is not pushed, it is not calculated; it happens like the snow falling from a branch under its own weight.

I witnessed another interesting case when I was working for Hennessy, the leading Cognac brand. The Japanese veteran leader of sales explained to me how Hennessy could enter the Japanese market in the 80s, and how it became so successful. The Japanese staff believed in the quality of high-end cognac made in France and conducted sales activities. However, Japanese wholesalers and liquor stores were not very enthusiastic about the idea of exploring the potential market, as in those days, most Japanese used to drink whisky and sake and did not know much about cognac. Still, Hennessy's staff did not give up. They were determined to promote cognac to end consumers. They personally visited exclusive clubs in the luxurious district of Ginza in Tokyo and suggested that they display Hennessy's bottles. Some clubs accepted their suggestion, as they wanted to offer their customers something new, like this high-quality liquor from France.

Soon, little by little, Hennessy started to sell. The customers who came to the exclusive clubs ordered cognac to entertain their clients. Suddenly, cognac was in demand. Neither the salesman of Hennessy, nor the owner of the clubs had thought this would happen. It was not because of the delicious taste of Hennessy cognac. It happened independently of the thinking of the sales team. The consumers ordered it because this expensive imported liquor represented status for themselves and their clients.

At that time, Japan was in the bubble economy and status items started to be sought after by more and more consumers. Once Hennessy became popular in Ginza, the clubs and shops in other areas became interested as well and, in no time, Hennessy achieved tremendous growth in the Japanese market. It became the number one market in the world.

When they experienced this phenomenon, Hennessy staff finally recognized, "We are not selling cognac, we are selling status." This movement of the consumers happened naturally, without planning, and as a result of the passion of the sales team for their high-quality products and brand. As it is said in Kyudo, the natural release cannot be planned. This natural release is similar to what Peter Drucker observed when he said, "The customer rarely buys what the company thinks it's selling."

For premium brands and retail business, it is essential to create the authentic quality of the product, brand and store so that it sells, instead of the company and the sales team trying hard to 'flog' it. With the advent of a digital age, millennials are becoming even more sensitive to the attitude of companies, and they instantly pull back when they feel that a company is pushing a product on them. In stores, one must control the desire to sell and be patient enough to allow the sale to happen. Focus on the feelings of the customer, not on your own desire to sell. This is the number one rule of sales.

From time to time, I still think of the moment when 'A Grand Aventure' was sold. I was engrossed in the conversation with the customer and then, all of a sudden, this high-end item was sold. It was as if the arrow left me and hit the bull's eye as soon as I became selfless. The reason I have been able to continue practicing Kyudo and business for so long is probably because they both give me these moments of spontaneous joy when there is a natural hit.

'A Grand Adventure' train sculpture,
limited edition by Lladro.

ONE SHOT
AT A TIME

6

Forget about the previous shot.
You cannot repeat a successful experience.

APPOINTING GLOBALLY ACTIVE DESIGNERS

Kyudo has a principle of concentrating on one shot at a time. This means that the archer is encouraged to take each shot without thinking of the one before or the one after. In practice, we learn that this is actually quite difficult. During the tests from the 4th dan onwards, we usually need both arrows to hit the target. If we shoot well with the first arrow, we instantly feel so close to executing a successful performance that we naturally try to remember how we did so well and repeat our first successful shot. This distraction generates analytical thinking and thus prevents us from executing a good and fluid shot the second time. So, the teacher encourages us to start each shot with a completely fresh mind and to throw away the memory of the prior shot. At first, I found that I was struggling with this approach. In general, I feel much safer when I am in control and I know in advance what I am going to do. The teacher smiled and insisted that I stop worrying; he said, "Your body will remember the way to shoot properly." Even if on the test day I am still struggling to shoot, I strive to build my self-confidence by trusting that my body will understand what to do.

The essence of this practice gave me some useful hints in business management. When applied to business, the principle of taking one shot at a time means to start each new year with a fresh new idea. The previous year may have been a success, but simply repeating the same strategy shows that you are not placing importance on each new year. With Godiva, we could take on a similar strategy to try and repeat the success of the previous year. But in a mature market, if we create the same product each year, selling in the same packages, then the customer will become bored with our products. It is only natural for the customer to think, "I gave Godiva's chocolate as a gift last year, so I want to buy a different brand this year." This is especially the case between married couples and those in long-term relationships, where many people do not want to give the same gift repeatedly.

Every year Godiva had been coming up with new types of chocolates and new types of packaging for special occasions, including Valentine's Day, even before I became the president. But not many customers were aware of this. Packaging designs were created by the in-house design team so, even though they were creating new designs, they had a similar look and feel each year

This led us to decide to outsource the designs to world-renowned artists. I figured that if the looks were drastically different, the customer would notice that the chocolate inside was different as well.

For the first two years, we asked Jaime Hayon, a world famous Spanish designer who was chosen as one of the 100 representative modern creators in *TIME* magazine (2007), to undertake the designs. In 2014, it was Nathalie Lete, a very popular French illustrator who does colourful and stylish artwork. In 2015, it was Studio Job, an up-and-coming design unit from Antwerp, Belgium who had swept up recognition and received all kinds of design awards worldwide. In 2016, it was Charlotte Gastaut, an illustrator who created designs for Hermès and L'Occitane. In 2017, it was the American artist Sara Frieden who had worked for *Times Magazine* and the *Village Voice*.

Outsourcing the designs made each package look totally new and fresh. And this collaboration between the world's top designers and our in-house design team gave fresh inspiration to each member of our team, and empowered them to manage the whole creation process in a new way each year.

This approach worked because our customers are happy to recieve this year's limited edition design and they know that the next year they will again have something different to discover.

I feel strongly that it is so important for those of us who do business to take one shot at a time and start each year with a fresh mind, being aware of the latest changes in the market and continuously offering new products and services.

THE TRAP CALLED 'THE COMFORT ZONE'

In order to grow our Valentine's sales every year, we need to continually create new chocolate and new packaging. This puts me under great pressure when looking for new designers and unveiling the Valentine's chocolate package each year. Once we make a decision on the designer, I cannot help but worry, "Were they the best choice? Will we produce another success?"

But to worry about an action that has been done does not create any new fruitful outcomes. It just prevents us from moving forward with a positive energy. The practice in the workplace of the Kyudo principle of 'one shot at a time' helps me to live better with the decisions and actions that I am taking. I reflect that each shot is new and, when one arrow has left the bow, we can never take it back or repeat the same shot. I do not need to judge myself and feel guilty because of a poor shot. I did my best with my ability at the moment of that specific shot. Now, I just have to shoot a new arrow with my best intent and effort. This is easier to do in the archery hall, as each shot is a physical action and the new shot immediately replaces the old one. In the workplace, most of our actions are decisions that are mental in nature, so that they stay much longer in the mind than an archery shot. Nevertheless, the practice of 'one shot at a time' taught me that in the workplace also there is no benefit from thinking about an arrow that has already left the bow.

Once we succeed, those around us expect even greater success. Many succumb to this type of psychological pressure and tend to take the safe route of doing the same thing each year. But unless you overcome these worries you will not find the courage to move on to the next step. In order to counteract this hesitation, I always remind myself of another lesson that I have learned in Kyudo: you have to push yourself beyond your comfort zone in order to grow.

When taking up a new challenge, anyone can fall into worrying whether or not this was the right choice. There is the urge to retreat into your comfort zone. But you should never go back there. Your new attempt may not feel comfortable, but it is still a necessary step for your growth. In Kyudo, we are taught to always aim for a higher spiritual and technical state. The teacher guides you to each of these levels and gives you a technical goal to work on. Each successive goal means discovering a better way to use every part of your body but, when we try this, our body and mind are prone to resisting change because we feel clumsy doing something new. In addition, when we try to succeed, we find a sudden drop in accuracy in hitting the target. So, when something new is taught, there is the powerful temptation not resist putting it into practice, because we do not want to push beyond our comfort zone or risk the unfamiliar due to the potential for making mistakes. When people are faced with these types of situations, they choose one of these two paths:

1. Listen to the teacher and challenge themselves to go on to the new stage, or,
2. Ignore the teacher politely and continue with their comfortable way of shooting.

Over the years, students that choose the first path are the ones that progress to the higher levels, even if this takes more time to allow for adjustment periods when they are out of their comfort zone. The pupils who choose the second path may sometimes be the most naturally skilled but, over the long term, they finally get stuck at a certain level and cannot progress.

The same challenge is true with business, both at individual and company levels.

For the individual, the role of the teacher to guide us to our next stage can involve the executive coach or the 360-feedback process from our boss, colleagues and subordinates that many corporations put in place. As we cannot see ourselves in our business daily actions – in the same way that we cannot see our own form while shooting – we need a mirror to reveal our blind spots. Once we become aware of these, it is up to us to decide to make the effort to stop a bad habit and acquire a new one. As Kyudo taught us, getting rid of bad habits and acquiring new positive ones requires constant discipline and follow up, because progress tends to happen very slowly and this is not a linear development path: there may be many forward and backward steps before a new stage is reached and then stabilized.

A new job experience can also be a way to grow. This may be a new project that we volunteer to lead or a different position in the organization that requires a more challenging skill set than our existing role. For example, in multinationals, when someone applies for a position of responsibility in an unfamiliar country, this can provide an experience out of the comfort zone, allowing the potential for new obstacles and, therefore, greater progress and growth. This challenge can be recognized later on as the development step that leads to a more significant leadership position. The significance of taking on a new challenge will often have the pleasant advantage of increasing status or regard within the company, even though this may not always be the primary 'target' of the move.

At the company level, when sales are going well, everyone wants to stay in that comfort zone and they prefer not to push beyond it and try something new. Companies that have been at the top of their industry, in particular, do not actively seek to attempt new things. However, what has made them successful up until that point is not what will push them to new successes in the future, especially in these times when the pace of change has never been so fast. Top management should make it their priority to ask staff, "What's next? What will be improved and what will change?" They should then use this to take on a new challenge. When everything is going well and sales are growing, that is an opportunity to try something new. As in Kyudo, this new encounter might feel uncomfortable or deliver less profitability in the beginning, but this is essential in order to evolve into the next stage of growth. If this step is not taken then there is a danger that, when the sales growth slows down to the point where it is almost flat, then the top management will not have the strength or finances to start something new.

Japanese companies have had many shining successes, but they can be a burden for the next generation. The history of the ups and downs of companies – for example the recent troubles in the electronics sector for Sharp and Panasonic – shows this clearly. Some companies with wonderful past performances have deteriorated and this decline can mainly be attributed to two factors. One is that the organization has built upon a particular success and has becomes conservative, as the top management is not challenging the status quo. The other is that the tasks and responsibilities for middle management have become routine. In other words, the whole organization cannot step out of their comfort zone. In Kyudo it is said that your body remembers your shooting, as years of practice build physical habits, good and bad, in the way you draw the bow. The company also has a 'body' in the sense that the organization is an organism that has built various habits and processes. It 'remembers' its own way of manufacturing and distributing products as well as how to make a profit. But in these habits – including the ones that are labelled 'good' because of having led to past financial achievements – resides the inertia that prevents engagement with new strategies that might lead to further future success.

You cannot afford to rest on past accomplishments. You ought to take another step towards the unknown and shoot another arrow. Endless effort is also the Way in the corporate world. This should be taken to heart as we face our customers with a fresh mind each time.

STUDY WHERE YOUR ARROW LANDS

7

Business improves not only through a 'hit' or 'miss', but also by studying the cause.

THINKING ABOUT THE OUTCOME

Kyudo teaches us to look at 'yadokoro'. Yadokoro means 'where the arrow lands'. You can move close to the target and study it carefully to find where, at what angle, and how your two arrows landed. Sometimes, they are far apart from each other; sometimes they closely miss the target. At this point, you must think about why they landed the way that they did and explore the influencing factors; you then take responsibility for what happened and take the effort to make technical improvements for your next shot. That's what looking at yadokoro is all about. It sounds like a natural process but, in our everyday life, it is not so easy to practice. We tend to look at the target only to see the outcome – whether it hit or it missed – without analyzing the cause.

It is a healthy practice to look at yadokoro in business. When I became the president of Godiva, our overall sales were growing. But with deeper analysis, I could see that sales in the same stores had been consistently dropping over the past three years. Examining things further, we found that the number of customers going to each store was decreasing. This showed that the attractiveness of our shops, products, and brand was weakening.

Godiva is world-famous for being a pioneering high-end chocolate brand. Brand awareness was over 90% in Japan, so the decline in footfall could not have been due to a lessened rate of awareness. The waning of sales could only be attributed to the fact that the brand was becoming less relevant to consumers.

The more famous a brand is, the more pride the management and employees have in their brand. This makes it very difficult to admit to a decrease in a brand's attractiveness. It takes humility and courage. Companies have to accept the fact, reflect on it, and make an effort to take new actions, which will instigate change. Godiva had to do the same. So we decided to revitalize the brand by renewing our stores, products, and our communication strategy with the customer. By studying and practicing yadokoro, we were able to find the cause and problems, and saw that there were areas that needed to be improved. We focused on improving the following four points:

1. **Making our shops accessible and appealing so that customers would want to return.** The shops were redesigned and made brighter. We deviated from the more dignified brown colour palate we previously used and made our display more vibrant. The shops that had been using the same show cases and shelves for years were completely renewed. This was very effective. Without changing the locations of the shops, we were able to increase our sales by 20% year on year.

2. **Offering a wider range of products and prices.** Godiva had an established image of being a high-end brand, which dissuaded younger people somewhat. So we offered a wider variety of wrapped chocolates in the lower price range, as well as products in cute packages for casual gifts.

3. **Focusing our energy on developing new products for the summer, which is typically a slow season.** As we analysed the sales figures, it was plain to see that our sales took a nosedive between April and September. This was because of the hot weather at this time of the year. When it is hot, eating chocolate is not as desirable as it is at other times of the year. In order to combat this, we accelerated product development on new summer sweets such as chocolate-based ice cream, a cold chocolate drink (the 'Chocolixir'), and baked goods.

4. **Running TV commercials in order to actively communicate the deliciousness of our products.** Godiva had been using street signs and print media for advertising, but they had not proven very effective. Photos lacked the movement and texture necessary to draw out the desire of eating chocolates. We decided to run TV commercials,

which focused on appealing to the appetite through a sophisticated eating scene, which could better capture the immediate sensory appeal and convey the attractiveness of the products to the customer, helping motivate them to make a purchase. We stopped using other platforms for advertising and invested our entire promotion budget into TV commercials. In general, luxury brands such as Godiva do not run TV commercials. The platform of TV is known to be effective for mass-market merchandising. But we aimed to firstly entice the audience to visit our shops so that we could increase our customers. We wanted the customers to re-realize (via TV commercials) how delicious, high-quality, and stylish Godiva's chocolates are.

All these strategies contributed to our success and saw an increase in the number of repeat customers. Since 2011, same-store sales have recovered and have even been steadily growing. The sales increased because we looked beyond the figures and analysed the reasons behind the decline, before providing solutions that could lead to a better outcome.

INVESTIGATING THE CAUSE AND FINDING THE CULPRIT ARE DIFFERENT THINGS

We need to examine the result and search for its cause in order to make improvements to move on to the next level.

When I joined Godiva Japan, many people told me, "The Japanese don't have a custom of eating a lot of chocolate; the economy is growing at 1% rate per year, so sales won't grow that much." These comments came from looking at the surface figures. They were not derived through analyzing the market to discover the real cause. Therefore, the conclusions were drawn using misrepresentative data. This led to misleading results.

People like looking at successful outcomes, but do not enjoy exploring the causes for failure. However, in order to move forward, it is important to analyse and explore the cause of the failure. Failures and troubles are wonderful opportunities to investigate the causes, with a view to making solid improvements.

However, in Japan, cultural niceties present problems for this type of approach. Although people start off with the intention of seeking the cause of failure, too much concern and consideration for others and their positions in the organization becomes an obstacle. They then do not follow through with the full analysis, and stop the process before they discover the real cause of the problem. There have been times that my colleagues have said that we should solve the problem instead of seeking out the cause because identifying the cause will result in placing blame on an individual, and will lead to embarrassment.

However, I am not looking for a culprit; I am simply seeking out the cause in an impartial way. In Kyudo, the teacher always guides the student to identify the cause of the failure in shooting. The teacher is not inhibited by feelings of being 'nice' to the student. Both teacher and student know that Kyudo is a practice where the 'truth' in shooting should be pursued.

Finding out what caused something is the shortest path to a solution. If you do not properly analyse and identify the concern, due to consideration for others, then you cannot solve the core problem, which will not bring good results for the company or for the employees. Even if it seems that a problem has been solved, if the cause is still there, the same problem will remain unresolved, time and again. This can eventually lead to the shareholders requesting a change of personnel and corporate restructuring.

Shifting personnel is an easy solution when a company is faced with serious problems. It is a sad result of not having done the right analysis and not having re-adjusted direction and strategy at the right time. But if we are to take the approach of looking at the yadokoro (where the arrow lands), then we would focus on the process of re-adjusting direction, rather than placing *blame* on different individuals. When I joined Godiva, sales growth was slowing down, but I continued with the same leadership team as before, and did not re-shuffle. It was the same team that had been working in management from before; collectively we hammered out a new strategy and plan of action, and led the company to great success.

It is often the case that, when a company is in financial crisis, the employees are already aware of where the problems lie and what caused them. The employees on site – in particular the sales personnel – have a good grasp of the reasons why sales are poor and the problems that the company faces, since they are the closest to the consumer. They see and feel the cause of such problems every day. Why do companies end up facing a crisis when there are people inside the company who are aware of and understand where the problems lie? The answer is that top management often fail to listen to the truth and take the proper steps at the right time to prevent a crisis.

The first thing they should do is to create an atmosphere where the employees feel encouraged to seek out the cause of the problems, and where they can freely share their own opinions and analysis without worrying about the pressure and possible punishment for doing so, and without concern about politeness or social niceties.

Secondly, after seeking out the cause and making a decision on a solution, top management should secure the budgets and resources required to take action and find the solution. Although we may pay more attention to the ostentatious sales activities instead of the pragmatic problem-solving activities, we should continue with these down-to-earth improvements consistently.

These two actions are a part of looking at yadokoro in business. In order to avoid a crisis, we should make a habit of seeking out the cause. This can be achieved by looking backwards from the outcome, instead of focusing the mind solely on the problem.

OPENING
YOUR HEART

8

Adapting to changes in current times, while
protecting the DNA of established business.

GODIVA AS AN ESTABLISHED BUSINESS

Godiva is a world-renowned chocolate company. Its history goes all the way back to 1926, when chocolatier Pierre Draps began making pralines in his confectionery workshop in Brussels.

While he put all his creativity into making delicious chocolate, his wife, who had an excellent artistic sense, came up with the idea of putting the chocolates in elegant boxes and selling them as a gift. It was a breakthrough idea, as in those days, each piece of chocolate was generally sold separately. Chocolates packaged in beautiful golden boxes became very popular, and their company made leaps in progress and sales.

In 1945, they changed their company's name from 'Chocolaterie Draps' to 'Godiva', because the Draps family was inspired by the legend of Lady Godiva. Lady Godiva was an 11th century noblewoman married to the powerful Lord of Coventry in England. She asked him many times to lessen the burden of taxes for the people, which he refused to do. Ultimately, he told her he would lower taxes only if she rode naked on horseback through the town. Determined to help the people, she went to the town on a horse, with nothing but her long hair to cover herself. The people of Coventry were requested to remain inside their homes. Her husband kept his word and reduced the taxes for the people. Values associated with Lady Godiva such as boldness, generosity, and a pioneering spirit still inform Godiva's essence today. Godiva has grown into a global premium brand, with more than 600 shops in more than 100 countries around the world. Over the years, there have been many people involved in building the Godiva tradition and who have solidified its position as an established business.

DNA OF AN ESTABLISHED BRAND

As an established business, one of the most important missions is to maintain tradition. Established businesses in Japan, however, seem often to *only* focus on maintaining tradition, at the expense of other important factors. True tradition should not only value a company's history, but should constantly renew itself for the future. Innovation of established companies is born when they can maintain the tradition and the DNA of the brand, while not becoming mired in the past. This allows the company to stay open to new ideas and to meet the needs of the changing times.

Kyudo has had its innovations too. It has been passed down from master to apprentice via 'kuden' (oral teaching or instruction) over the years. Kyudo is very different from any Western art or sport, in that we do not need to devise our own new way of thinking or methodology. We learn the ways of a tradition that has been passed down for many generations and aim for the ideal shooting according to this tradition. We can express ourselves not through creating something new, but through learning the conventions and traditions properly. It is as Confucius said in *Analects*: "I have transmitted what was taught to me without making up anything of my own." However, you may wonder if thinking like this will ever provide room for anything new or innovative.

Although Kyudo's tradition has been passed down through ages, it did go through innovation during the Edo period (1602-1867). The Edo period was an age of peace. The era of warfare and using bows and arrows had ended; therefore Kyudo became a form of training of the body and mind. Until that point, the enemy had been external, but now it was *inside* the individual. The art evolved into a struggle with oneself.

If Kyudo hadn't kept up with the changes throughout the years, then it would have been replaced by other sports (perhaps Western archery) and disappeared. But Japanese archery adjusted to the peaceful times and survived as Kyudo, the training of the self.

Traditions can be innovated upon and developed further, if they are willing to make adjustments to fit the changes seen over the years.

When I joined Godiva, the employees had a strong awareness that Godiva was a luxury brand. This factor was very important. But if we had been fixated upon the idea that our shops had to be in the same location as other luxury brands, then our customers would have had to travel a great distance in order to buy some chocolates, which might have seemed off-putting. As a result of this realization, we then tried a new idea of selling Godiva products at convenience stores. This was part of the realization of the strategy of making Godiva an accessible and aspirational brand.

When we decided to sell Godiva chocolates, and Valentine's Day and White Day products, at 7-Eleven, some people were opposed to the idea because they felt that it would damage the brand's image. But, without this step, customers who lived in an area that did not have access to Godiva shops could only buy our products through the internet. We wanted those customers to have easier access to our brand and enjoy a sense of luxury. We made an arrangement so that our customers at convenience stores could receive the product in the same Godiva shopping bags as they would in our Godiva shops. This made it a more luxurious experience for our customers. For convenience stores, this arrangement was unheard of, but they accommodated our request. This proved to be a successful sales strategy. We were able to increase sales in all the other sales channels as well. Twenty years ago, it was difficult for a premium brand to expand their sales channels, but with the evolution of the customer's shopping behaviour and lifestyle, the situation has now changed drastically. We called our channel expansion 'luxury by the moment'. This expressed that an instant of luxury is independent from the channel used to convey it.

The job of an established business is not only to maintain tradition, but also to be open-minded and fulfil the ever-changing needs of the customer, as well as offering convenient products and services.

Each established business has its DNA. This DNA is comprised of the unique features and ways of thinking which only successful businesses have. With Godiva, these are: high-quality chocolates, special recipes by chefs, beautiful packaging, and bringing happiness via chocolate. Though we may change our products, sales channels, and the atmosphere of our shops according to the needs of the times, this DNA is timeless. This is the heart and soul of the established brand, and is something essential that has been continually alive since the founding of the business.

The true approach of an established business should be to respond to the changing circumstances of the times, while preserving its DNA. In the luxury industry, famous turnarounds such as Dior, Saint Laurent, Gucci, and Burberry have been made when the management search for the DNA of the brand in its history and archives, and then reinterpret the essence of the brand with a new creative approach, to fit with the present epoch.

Things are changing rapidly in the 21st century. An established company can lose their market share and go out of business, unless they are able to maintain a loyal perspective towards the organization's history and past, and yet are flexible enough to accept the changes of the current times. In addition, the changes that give tremendous power to the consumers can present wonderful opportunities for new growth for established businesses. Daring innovation is needed in order to preserve tradition.

"I was born in chocolate... It has seduced me and I have dedicated myself all my life to this art. I have lived a wonderful dream."
Pierre Draps (1919-2012)

THE TARGET IS YOUR MIRROR

9

The customers outside your company are
the ones who evaluate your business.

THE JOYS OF HITTING THE TARGET

During the Japanese Edo period in the 17th century, the bow and arrow was a play toy for children. The excitement of aiming and hitting the target captivated young imaginations. It was also a means to cultivate important virtues in children such as patience, soul-searching, and effort.

Adults also have joyous moments in Kyudo practice, whether they are beginners or advanced students. These come when they do their best to shoot properly – when the arrow flies straight to the target and strikes it with a sharp sound. This is an exciting and happy moment for children and adults alike.

Unfortunately, once we become adults and enter the business world, we tend to forget about the sense of fun we had as children. This is because we are pressured by time, sales figures, and the command to perform; therefore we lose sight of the real purpose of our endeavours. We should exert ourselves with the aim of performing "for the good of the work to be done and for nothing else", as explained by A.K Coomaraswamy in *Christian and Oriental Philosophy of Art*.

If we can think of business as a way of servicing the customer, a whole new world opens up. It gives us a sense of fun, much like hitting the target in Kyudo. When our customers are satisfied with our products and/or service, we feel the same joy and happiness as a result of our work as we would when hitting the target at play. I believe that doing our best for the work to be done and maintaining this sense of playfulness is the key to leading businesses to success.

By practicing Kyudo, I have learned that you cannot see for yourself how you look when you shoot the arrow. Since we cannot see for ourselves how we shoot the arrow, the target becomes the mirror, which shows us our reflection. The target is impersonal; it doesn't move. However, when we are at the stage of full draw before releasing the arrow, our mind moves with many intrusive thoughts and the target reveals our desires, weaknesses and worries. This mirror provides a clear image of our mental state, so that we may correct ourselves and do our best to reach a more stable level.

Similarly, in business we cannot step back and objectively see all our efforts as an organization. We need the consumer to reveal the strengths and weaknesses of the company. It is only when the customer purchases our products and services that we learn how they rate us and see the outcome of our actions.

In Kyudo, we often say: "The bow is our teacher. It never lies."

I think we can say the same in business: "The customer is our teacher. They never lie." The customer gives us an honest response and tells us what they liked right away. When we fail to deliver good products, they tell us where the problem was – if we are brave enough to investigate and identify the cause. Then, it is up to us to decide if we want to apply what we have learned to our business strategy or not. Sometimes, managers do not want to listen to the truth from the consumer and may credit the decline in sales to increased competition, or the economic environment, or another external factor. But, when sales decline, the consumer is simply reflecting that something is amiss within the company or its strategies.

In a corporate organization, the power of hierarchy often creates an atmosphere where employees at lower levels and sales staff in stores may sometimes feel or think that they cannot freely express themselves. Owing to lack of time and power, and other organizational restraints, they tend to simply listen to those higher up.

In this type of culture, it is easy to depend only on outside professionals such as research companies to listen to the customers and observe them. However, marketing data alone is insufficient. Managers also need to go out there themselves and obtain the live data, which provides the 'real voice' of the customers. This information should then be passed on to those in charge of marketing and sales, but also to top management. Listening to real voices helps to generate feedback from outside the company and to shape the sales and marketing actions that you need to perform within the corporate organization. It is only when data and the real voice become one that we can really grasp the valuable message that the customer is telling us through their actions.

Based on this experience, at Godiva, we started the 'Customer's Voice Project'. This project involves inviting the manager and staff of each shop to our Tokyo Office, in turn, to deliver the voice of customers at a round-table conference. Marketing and merchandising people guide the meeting and simply ask questions of the sales staff about the recent launches of products and advertising campaigns. During these meetings, we never refer to sales performance. The managers and staff share with us at the Head Office what they have heard from the customers: their likes and requests, and what they themselves felt from serving and interacting with the customers. The staff feel free to speak up in this atmosphere of openness and blameless honesty, and each of them is very passionate in relaying real words from the customers. The discussion sometimes digresses in many directions but, if we listen carefully to each of the voices, we can sometimes discover moments of truth that will help us in generating our future plans for products and promotion. Personally, I love the atmosphere of these conferences, which are full of consumer insights and laughter from the sales staff. When I attend, I feel that we are creating a vital link, an invisible line of continuity between our head office, who conceive and promote products, and the customers who buy them. It reminds me of what I have been taught in my Kyudo practice, of how we should look at the target: it is not just about technically aiming to the centre of the target, but sending our energy to the target to create a vital connection.

Godiva has more than 288 shops in Japan and, as a retail business, it is a competitive advantage to establish a listening system where we can hear the voices of the field and create a dynamic relationship with our customers from all our shops.

LISTENING TO THE VOICE OF THE CUSTOMER

Before we started the Customer's Voice as a formal project, there was an incident which made us realize once again how important it is to listen to the customer. This was with regard to a product called 'Keepsake', which is part of our Valentine's Day series. The product is an assortment of chocolates in a cute little case.

Soon after I had joined Godiva, the sales of this product ranked in the 50th position among all the Valentine's Day products. However, in listening to one of the sales staff and reading over the questionnaires, we learned something unexpected: many people said they were buying it as a gift to themselves. After they ate the chocolate, some customers were collecting the cases and using them as trinket boxes because we were redesigning these each year. We didn't suggest or propose it, but they gained enjoyment out of using the empty box as a keepsake container. So, we learned that Keepsake has enthusiastic fans. This information taught us two important points: first, that during the Valentine's Day season, some people give themselves Godiva chocolates as a reward. The second was that the customers value packaging that can have its own use after they have eaten the chocolates.

We decided to set two themes for Valentine's Day and ran TV commercials accordingly. One was a Valentine's Day gift for someone special to you. The other was a Valentine's Day gift for yourself. To promote this consumer occasion of a gift for yourself we named this campaign 'My Godiva'. We promoted it through TV commercials and visual merchandising, always highlighting the name 'My Godiva'. The product of this campaign was the keepsake. When it was featured on TV, it looked beautiful – like a jewel – so attractive that everyone would want to purchase it for themselves as a reward. It won the hearts of women and it sold out in no time. It was our target – our customers – that helped us to realize the value of the keepsake and to come up with the My Godiva campaign. This, in turn, helped to turn the Keepsake into a star item in its own right. The Keepsake then ranked as our 5th product.

The joy of hitting the target was also evident in another campaign titled, 'Love & Hug' in 2013, where we set up a life size gentleman-like doll in front of our shops and, as female customers hugged this doll, the strength of her love was quantified by the strength of her hug. Some of the employees were concerned and said, "The Japanese don't have a custom of hugging like the Americans and the Europeans do. I don't know if Japanese ladies would accept and appreciate this campaign." But once the campaign started, many customers lined up in front of each shop and a great number of ladies hugged this gentleman doll. The campaign became a hot topic on social networks too and was a huge success in creating consumer engagement and traffic into our stores. This is an example where the arrow was released and it had hit the bull's-eye; we all shared the fun of it together.

The business environment of the 21st century is a unique one. About 30 years ago, the leaders in the market were big manufacturers. The consumers' options were limited and it was difficult to purchase various types of products. But now, even if you do not have any stores nearby, it is very easy to buy the products from all over the world that fulfil your needs via the internet.. The market is becoming more and more transparent and the customers are calling the shots, while in the past the power was in the hands of the manufacturers. This means that the market is increasingly becoming a faithful mirror of the company's actions. Japan is one of the most advanced consumption markets in that respect, where the frequency of launching of new products is one of the highest in the world. When you launch a new product, the Japanese consumers react immediately. For each new launch, the market will reflect success or failure like the 'moon reflected in the water'.

You can clearly see, and very quickly, whether it is a hit or a miss.

YOUR LIFE AND YOUR SHOOTING ARE THE SAME

10

What's important in both Kyudo and business is improving your life and shaping your character. Something is always born out of the challenge.

WHAT I LEARNED FROM FAILING AT KYUDO

I hold the rank of 5th dan in Kyudo. I also hold the first grade of teacher, which is called Renshi. The kanji of Renshi is made up of the two ideograms: 'ren' 練 which means 'train' or 'polish', and 'shi' 士 which means 'samurai' and also 'scholar'. There are two other teaching grades above Renchi, which are Kyoshi (the ideogram 'kyo' conveys the notion of 'teaching' and 'doctrine') and Hanshi, which is the highest teaching grade and designates a master (the ideogram 'han' means 'model'). The Renshi title is given to those who meet the following qualifications:

1. Firm in character and has the ability to teach Kyudo. More-over, there should be evidence of technical advancement above the previous levels.
2. Holds the 5th dan.

You may think that I am boasting about this title, but I struggled for a long time in order to achieve this result. I have historically been a clumsy student of Kyudo.

It has been 27 years since I started practicing Kyudo. In the beginning, it was a lot of fun as I was learning and improving, and taking a grade examination every so often, and I was very happy when I passed these. The move up to 3rd dan was a fairly steady progress for me, as I experienced successes at my 1st and 2nd dan exams.

However, once I reached the 3rd dan, I found it difficult to pass the next exam to move from 3rd to 4th dan. Each time I took this particular exam, I reflected upon the previous exam and what I had done wrong. I took the next exam with a fresh mindset; and yet I kept failing each time.

It is said that in the Way of the Bow, anyone – even the most gifted – will encounter an insurmountable wall at some point in the course of their practice. But to face such a wall just three years after I started Kyudo was an unpleasant surprise for me.

In France, I had always been a straight-A student and always ranked at the top or second in school. I never failed to pass exams, so I could not understand why I was repeatedly failing the same exam. I had applied 15 times to the 4th dan examination... and failed 15 times. This was a totally new experience for me; it was quite shocking. My self-esteem and confidence were seriously hurt.

I first thought that maybe there was an unspoken rule that you must fail the examination to advance from 3rd dan to 4th dan many times before you can pass it. But I watched the attempts of my peers and observed that some passed it after only a few tries. I had to admit that my failure was owing to the fact that I simply hadn't yet attained that level.

Observing how I was repeatedly failing, one old Kyudo teacher said to me, "Take the Kyudo examination, not in order to pass it, but in order to learn about yourself."

These words greatly changed my values. This was the beginning of a 'metanoia', a change of mind or intellectual metamorphosis, as A. K. Coomaraswamy describes in his essay, "On being in one's right mind".

Up until this point, I had been raised on the cultural values of my parents and teachers, who expected me to pass all exams. This was the single track of thinking: you have to pass an exam and achieve results to become a valued member of society. When I took the entrance exam for university and job interviews, the only thing I desired was to pass. So, repeatedly failing to pass the Kyudo exam was a failure in my mind, and I was discouraged and angry at myself for some time. I started to look for faults, such as the idea that I was probably failing the exam repeatedly because of a technical problem I had, like not straightening my right hand at 'hanare' (release). Maybe I had other problems as well.

Why do I keep failing? I kept asking myself this question, as I was going through these failings. The Kyudo path that I chose freely was very different from my business career, where I had to look for a job, bring deliverables, aim for a better salary, or please a demanding boss. No one had ordered me to learn and practice Kyudo. No one was pressuring me to take the Kyudo examination. Then why was I taking this same exam again and again and failing each time? Why I was so depressed when I failed this exam?

To answer these questions, I needed to think back to why I had got involved in Kyudo in the first place. Soon after entering the corporate world I began to feel the normal frustrations of work: the pressures of the hierarchy, of colleagues and of clients. Events did not go always the way I wanted, and there were always some business and relationship obstacles that surfaced, for which I did not have all the solutions. A few years later, I discovered Kyudo, which would provide me with a self-development path deeply engrained in authentic tradition. I believed that I was starting Kyudo with a pure mind and, since there were no expectations or constraints from society, I envisioned that the path would be smooth and fulfilling, and one that would effectively counterbalance the challenges of the corporate world. I did not at all expect for Kyudo to bring me similar frustrations to those which I faced in my working life.

The path of the exams and my repeated failures taught me that the negative and positive emotions I faced had nothing to do with external factors, but that these were an inherent part of my character that I had to deal with.

As Kyudo is a solitary pursuit, without opponents, it reflects entirely on what you do, without interference from others. So there is no excuse to look for. Because of this, I finally started to understand the core essential teaching of Kyudo: that your shooting and your life are the same (Sha Soku Jinsei).

In Kyudo, what is on your heart – worry, desire, confidence, calmness – is reflected in the momentum with which the arrow leaves the bow, and in how it hits the target. When you become aware of your weaknesses through witnessing the tangible aspects of your shooting, you can take the proper measures to correct and improve. This process is what Kyudo teachers call 'a fight against yourself' (jibun to no tatakai). A. K. Coomaraswamy in the essay mentioned previously alludes to this internal fight, when he quotes from the *Maitri Upanishad* (VI, 34-6): "The mind is said to be twofold pure and impure: impure, by connection with desire, pure by separation from desire."

Since gaining a better understanding of this, whenever I fail exams or cannot improve the technical aspects of my shooting, I take time to meditate on *why* I started Kyudo. The purpose of doing Kyudo for me was not to become a master, but to follow the path of Kyudo, to learn, to do my best, and to polish my mind and heart. In realizing this, I also accepted the fact that I was clumsy. Meditating at these times helps me to centre my mind; it reminds me of why I started doing Kyudo and has helped me to cease from worrying about the exams.

There are some people who study Kyudo and yet they are against attempting the tests, as they believe that aiming to pass the tests results in encouraging the pursuit of the grades and, thus, the growth of the ego. They believe that the purity of the practice should not be mixed with the pursuit of external signs of success.

However, as we have said, the traditional approach of Kyudo is to encourage the passage of the tests, as a training of the self. It is precisely *because* there is an obstacle and a desire to pass the test, that the archer can recognize within himself how his heart is still full of desires and wishes of recognition.

In the corporate world, you don't have clear and regular events similar to an examination where you can clearly identify success or failure. But you can still decide if you are ready to take a risk in testing yourself, by raising your hand for a project or a position that has a clear role and responsibility. In doing so, success and failure will become manifest to you.

A GOOD SHOT SEEN AS A GIFT

One day, my Kyudo teacher, Hiroko Uragami, said to me, "Your shooting has improved and changed almost frighteningly." I can never forget these words of praise, especially the words 'improved... almost frighteningly'. I received these words when I was practicing at my regular practice hall (dojo) in the suburbs of Tokyo, a few days after I finally passed the examination of 4th dan on my sixteenth attempt.

My special state of mind that had 'almost frighteningly' improved my techniques lasted for about a month. The technical flaws I had struggled with for years seemed to have all of a sudden disappeared. The release of my right hand became sharp and natural. My mind and my body were working in harmony. I had a completely new awareness and wonderful confidence in my Kyudo. But, then, oddly enough, after about a month, my old bad habits suddenly came back and I again lost my confidence.

This kind of experience is not limited to Kyudo. It is the same in life and business. When we pass the entrance exam to a university, when we receive a promotion, or when we get the job we wanted, we experience some moments of happiness and lightness, but then we soon encounter new obstacles.

In Kyudo, we use the term 'moratta sha' (a good shot seen as a gift) when we shoot an arrow better than normal. Some contribute this to luck and ability. However, I think that it is the reward for doing your best and continuing to challenge yourself. We do not know why it comes or when it will come, but when it does, everything starts working out smoothly and you can do what you have always wanted to do well.

After having passed the 4th dan, I found myself repeatedly failing at the examination for 5th dan. When I first started to take the 5th dan examination, my children were still very young and I did not pass the exam until they were students.

During this time, I changed companies three times and started to work for Godiva Japan.

On the day of the exam, I was waiting for my turn and stood in front of the target as I always did. I drew the bow and I was not thinking about passing the test, or about anything else. I performed my shooting with a pure heart. And then the arrow left the bow and I heard the sound of the arrow hitting the target.

Fifteen years had come and gone since I started to take the 5th dan exam. I couldn't help but feel that the god of Kyudo was watching over me and gave me 'moratta sha' (a good shot as a gift) on that day.

During these years, I found that it was not so much the goal of getting promoted to 5th dan that was so important to me, but rather putting forth my inner effort. And as you make that continual effort, 'moratta sha' will come to you.

Kyudo took its time to teach me so many things. The training of the formalized movements or etiquettes made me learn the value of respect, not only in the dojo, but also in the workplace. There is a saying in martial arts that says, 'Martial arts start with rei and end with rei'. 'Rei' is nowadays commonly translated as 'etiquette' or 'manner' and has also a functional meaning of 'making a bow'. The act of bowing is an integral part of the Japanese culture and through the physical act of bowing, a sentiment of respect is communicated to the other person. The Japanese culture believes that by adhering first to the outer form, this would also build adequately the inner sentiments. That is why many aspects of Japanese daily life may look so ritualized to a foreign observer, who may not immediately perceive the meaning behind the form. The ideogram 'rei' 礼 ('li' in Chinese) has also a deeper meaning and is an essential element of Confucianism, which stipulates that a social organization builds on proper etiquette according to one's role, responsibility and place, mirrors the ideal of the order and harmony of the universe. Influenced by Confucianism up to this day, Japanese companies follow forms of greetings and behaviours in the workplace: factors that contribute much to the harmony between employees.

In Kyudo it is said that you will not see improvement in shooting dignity (sha in) and the technical level of shooting (sha kaku) unless you strive to have integrity and dignity as a human being. Working on the heart and the mind through such techniques as Kyudo will enforce a discipline where you can see tangible results without self-delusion, as what you do and who you are constantly influencing each other.

In this respect, one of the most important things Kyudo taught me is that life will never be exactly the way I wish it to be. In Kyudo – as in life – you should never expect to hit the mark 100% of the time. The arrow does not always fly as you wish, and often misses the mark. If you aim at the target or try to make yourself look good, then the result will not be as you wished. As soon as you overcome one difficulty, you will face another. As you move up in dan ranking, you will face more difficult challenges, and things will be less and less as you wish.

I believe this to be the same in business. It is rare that something hits the mark as intended. And even when it does go well, you will encounter new challenges and be pursued by the desire to overcome them. That is all the more reason to make an effort on a daily basis: to accept gracefully that things will not always go as desired is a practice aimed at seeing outcomes as material for self-reflection and self-development. With this new mindset, the technique of the bow (kyujitsu) can become the Way of the Bow (Kyudo).

Likewise, the 'technique of management' can become the 'Way of management'. Management can be one of the noblest professions in this modern world if it is practised as a discipline, which aims at the development of the self and the coaching of others, as well as financial performance.

The Kyudo teaching: 'Your life and your shooting are the same' can inspire you to understand that 'your life and your business are the same'. Both Kyudo and business are journeys. When either does not go according to plan, the 'failure' provides the best time for self-reflection. When the arrow hits the bull's-eye, it is a moment of joy. Even when the journey is slow and full of obstacles, if we just continue to take steps one after another, we can learn and grow.

In both Kyudo and business, as long as the direction of the mind is focused on improvement, the effort is valuable and rewarding for both the inner man and the outer man that performs its tasks in the organization.

ORDINARY MIND IS THE WAY

In Kyudo practice, there is an important training of the mind that is called 'heijo shin,' which means an 'ordinary mind', a mind that remains self-possessed, impartial and peaceful, whatever the circumstances.

The expression heijo shin is composed of three characters:

1. 'Hei' means literally 'flat' or 'even' and has a figurative meaning of 'calm' or 'peaceful';
2. 'Jo' means 'ordinary' or 'always';
3. 'Shin' is the character for mind and heart. It has a broader meaning than just the rational and thinking mind, and designates also the emotions and feelings.

This is not a state of mind that is easy to maintain because, depending on our surrounding circumstances, we are all subject to thoughts and emotions of fear, excitement, surprise, confusion, and doubt. This 'ordinary mind' expression is often used in daily language in modern Japan: for example, mothers often advise their kids before going to a school examination to keep a 'heijo shin' mind, and to go to their examination place as if they would go to an ordinary day at school.

This ordinary mind teaching traces its origins to Chinese Taoism and Zen. The 19 Zen koan recorded in Mumonkan of the 9th century relates to a conversation between the Zen Master Nansen and the disciple Joshu:

"What is the Way (tao)?" Joshu asked Nansen.

"Ordinary mind (heijo shin) is the Way," answered Nansen.

In Kyudo, and other martial arts, we are taught to cultivate Heijo shin, so that we can face any situation with an ordinary mind, a mind that is calm and clear at all times. But how to come closer to this desirable state of mind? The answer is by practice.

The difficulty is that you do not become calm just because you *want* to. You have first to recognize that you are influenced by circumstances. Then you have to make continuous effort to train your mind every day as well as in unexpected circumstances, so that, gradually, the ordinary mind becomes part of you, even in extraordinary circumstances. In Kyudo, we become aware of the uncontrollable movements of our mind through two kinds of practice:

- The difference in our shooting at the 'makiwara' (a straw practice target that is shot from a bow's length away) and at the regular target that is at a distance of 28 meters. The form and movements that we can perform at the makiwara, especially at the critical moment of the release of the arrow, are usually much better than the ones we display in front of the real target.
- The difference in our shooting at our regular archery practice hall (dojo) and at the examination day and place.

The difference in performance between the regular place and the examination place in front of a jury is easy to imagine, but it is a puzzle for the archer to understand why, in the course of a regular practice day, he cannot shoot with exactly the same technical proficiency to both the makiwara and the target.

The learning is that the vital desire of the target is always there, even when we try earnestly to suppress it. It is preventing us from performing at our best.

An old teaching of Kyudo to overcome this obstacle is to practise with the following intention: 'Shoot to the makiwara as if you were shooting to the target' and 'shoot to the target as if you were shooting to the makiwara'.

Similarly, to overcome the unfamiliar circumstances of the Kyudo examination, it is advised to 'shoot every shot during the regular practice as if you were passing a test' and to 'shoot during the examination day as if you were shooting in your regular practice place'.

When I was applying to the Kyudo examinations, I discovered how difficult it was to embody 'heijo shin'. There are three periods of time where you can experience your attachment to the test or 'fruit of action' (as per the expression in the quoted verse of the *Bhagavad Gita*): the period before the shooting, the shooting itself, and after the shooting. As early as a few weeks before the test, I found out that I sometimes envisioned myself doing a wonderful shot and passing the examination. During the shooting itself, I have had times when I thought that I had an 'ordinary mind', but in fact my hands sweated at the moment of handling the bow and I performed a poor shot with tension. After the shooting itself, I often encountered intense feelings of sadness or joy, depending on my success or failure at the test.

To practise Heijo shin is a discipline where we make progress only little by little. It is a spiritual journey that is relevant for the man of action in this modern age. In *Bhagavad Gita*, the Hindu tradition calls it 'yoga': "Perform your duty, abandoning all attachment to success or failure. Such evenness of mind is called yoga."

This teaching is stressing the importance of approaching each action as it is in itself, without enveloping it with our wishes or fears, as born from the circumstances and expectations of others or the society.

In the workplace also, we can practice heijo shin. We are also going through many special circumstances, which put us out of balance with our ordinary mind. This can be a public speech, a presentation to an executive committee, a critical negotiation with clients or suppliers, an interview for a job, or a salary negotiation with our boss.

These are situations where we have a target in our mind, and we want to achieve a hit, and be a winner. These targets to hit naturally place us under tension, similar to that we might experience during an archery test. It is when there is a big gap between regular activities and important ones that stress builds inside us, because we have an important target we feel we must strive to hit.

The teaching from Kyudo is telling us that the way to practice ordinary mind in the workplace is to make the continuous effort to deal with every business action, such as a simple meeting with others, as if the outcome of such a meeting would be of critical importance for our business and career. Each target of each single day should be treated with a special importance, so that when the special day itself arrives, we will go through it with an ordinary mind.

PART 2

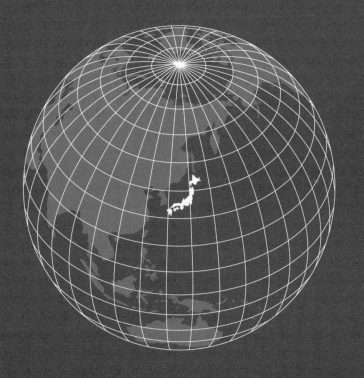

BUSINESS
IN THE LAND
OF JAPAN

LEARN THROUGH OBSERVATION

11

The Japanese are skilled in learning through observation; this is a skill that should be utilized in business.

THE MYSTERIOUS ABILITIES OF THE JAPANESE

In Kyudo there are three kinds of practice (keiko): 'kazu keiko', 'kufu keiko,' and 'mitori keiko'.

Kazu keiko is the repetition of shooting arrows many times. Kufu keiko is shooting each arrow while searching actively within yourself, through trial and error, how to realize technical forms with your own body. Mitori keiko (the etymology comes from the two characters of looking and taking) means to learn through observing with intense concentration how other archers shoot. This observation is not just visual, but by watching and understanding at the same time. Its value lies in the fact that it helps you to reflect on your own problems and to try to find a way to rectify these by seeing for yourself the style and technique of an advanced archer. From the foreigner's point of view, it is a rather mysterious practice method, because in the West, when you learn something, you start by first studying the theory.

The Japanese have an excellent ability to visually understand things, and that has much to do with the fact that kanji (Chinese characters) are used in Japanese writing. Kanji was originally derived from pictograms, and are ideograms that express meaning and ideas through visual symbols. The Japanese learn kanji from a young age and in doing so, acquire the skill of learning by observation. Many Japanese, however, do not realize that they have this unique ability. The alphabet that we Westerners use, on the contrary, is made up of a phonogram representing sound. The combinations of these sounds make up the meaning with etymological roots, but you cannot see and understand the meaning at a first glance at the alphabet letters. The thinking process is primarily logical and not visual.

This difference manifests itself very clearly in business meetings. Westerners discuss with logic the thoughts and concepts to the nth degree before we are convinced, while the Japanese do not get engaged by mere logical discussion.

They need to literally *see* what we are talking about, through means such as visual presentations or real products, to give their assent to the concept.

'Mitori keiko' is, I think, a very unique practice method developed by the Japanese, and is the art of observing and learning. This can be very useful in business.

It is crucial to observe in the field how your competitors are tackling tasks and, furthermore, how they are performing, so that you may learn from their example. It is also critical to observe silently the consumers who are buying their products. By so doing, you can sense the good qualities of your competitors, and then incorporate and practise them in your organization, in order to build new capabilities. This requires patience and focused observation, as in the archery hall. I call this practice 'mitori geiko in business'.

When I was the president of Lladro Japan, the brand was perceived as being very expensive and was known only by consumers interested in European luxury items. It was not viewed as relevant for mainstream consumers.

Also, in terms of size, the dolls were specifically designed for the larger houses in Spain. The smaller-scale housing typical in Japan made it difficult to have many of the dolls. For all of these reasons, sales in Japan were sluggish.

Soon after I joined, I started to research the Japanese market to see if there were occasions for buying figurines and display dolls. I found out that there was a beautiful custom on 3 March, which is the Japanese Doll Festival and Girls' Day. In major hotels on this day, I could see a set of ornamental dolls representing the Emperor, Empress, attendants and musicians in traditional court dress of the Heian period (794-1186). I asked my staff, "Why are we not more active in selling this type of doll?" The reply was, "Hina dolls are Japanese traditional items and people would not relate to European products."

I had doubts about that, and so I decided to go and visit the district of Asakusabashi where Japan's leading representative doll-makers are located. Although there is no custom to regularly purchase and display dolls in Japanese homes, these companies are very successful.

I talked to their staff and found that the majority of their sales were from ornamental dolls for the Girls' and Boys' Festivals, 'hina ningyo' (Hina dolls) and 'gogatsu ningyo' (May dolls). I learned that each family displays Hina dolls for the Girls' Festival on 3 March and May dolls and carp-shaped wind socks (koinobori) for the Boys' Festival on 5 May, as a token of their wish for their children's healthy growth. I also discovered that many of their products were just as expensive as Lladro's figurines.

The visit to Asakusabashi was a valuable 'mitori keiko' for me. I found out that there are people in the Japanese market who are willing to buy expensive dolls, if they are for the dolls' festivals.

I also visited the doll section of a department store. I asked the shop assistant, "What products are selling?" and he kindly explained the situation to me.

From all that he said, I learned that the luxurious set of Hina dolls displayed with accessories in several steps (dan kazari) take up too much space and are not suitable for modern Japanese housing; and that with the Westernization of housing, a pair of dolls of the emperor and empress (dairi-bina) is more popular, as they can be set up more easily in the living room space. In addition, I learned that recently people tended to prefer high-quality stylish dolls. I thought nothing would fulfil these needs better than Lladro's porcelain dolls.

I went back to my office and talked to the workers about all my findings, and yet the majority of them responded that even if the Spanish porcelain dolls entered the Japanese traditional market, they wouldn't be accepted by the consumers. Japan has its own culture: Japanese would not eat sushi in Tokyo made by the Spanish. This was their logic. This rationale would not convince me, as I knew, on the contrary, that some Japanese chefs had created delicious French and Italian cuisine and had opened excellent and successful restaurants in France and Italy.

I thought the Japanese would recognize and accept the Spanish dolls if they were genuine products of high quality. Lladro's Hina dolls were elegant, delicate, cute, and of good quality. Why wouldn't they sell?

WHY THE HINA DOLLS BORN IN SPAIN WERE A HUGE HIT

I decided to proceed to the next level of mitori keiko in business. What I observed convinced me to employ a careful strategy for the first year: we ran a full-page colour advertisement in a Japanese newspaper. The catch phrase was, "I celebrate with Lladro." It was targeted at stylish ladies who live in high-class apartment buildings. But some staff believed that we wouldn't be able to sell enough to recover the high costs associated with the advertisement.

However, I was confident that affluent ladies would desire Hina dolls that were suitable for their lifestyle. I was also convinced that Lladro's porcelain dolls, which can be displayed on low cabinets or tables, were exactly what was suitable to fulfil their desires.

The first newspaper advertisement was both a success and a failure. The success was that as soon as we ran the advertisement, we were swamped with orders. The failure was that we did not anticipate how great an impact the advertisement would have, and we went out of stock, the result being that many customers could not purchase the dolls after all. We received many complaints, which taught me how much the Japanese value these Festivals very highly, to celebrate their children's or grandchildren's growth.

The next year, we started the sales of Hina dolls and May dolls named 'Wakamusha' (young warrior) at the same time, and ran newspaper advertisements as well as a TV commercial. I recalled what the store assistant had said to me: "Grandparents are the ones who pay to buy the dolls, but the young parents are the ones who choose which ones to buy." With this advice in mind, we decided to focus on one TV station that was popular among the younger generation (24-29 years old). Our media target was towards the key decision makers and not the buyers themselves. In that respect, our approach was different from that of traditional Japanese dolls makers, who targeted grandparents.

As soon as TV commercials started, we received many inquiries, and Hina dolls started to sell immediately. And then the Wakamusha doll followed; we received order after order. A total of over 1,000 dolls were sold in no time. It was the first time in Lladro's history (over 60 years) that it had sold so many pricey products – 300,000 yen each – in such a short time.

This is a testimony to the success of our advertising strategy. Older generations tend to execute the decisions, but they want to make their children and grandchildren happy, so they listen to their requests, and on this occasion they gladly chose Lladro, as they learned about the high quality of its products.

At Lladro, we learned from Japanese humility and sincerity, and gave new value to the dolls for the Girls' and Boys' Festivals.

Mitori keiko in business can be a great source for generating new ideas. You learn by observing and studying, and then practise what you have learned.

A company should actively employ the skill of observing and learning as part of the business process. This is a skill that the Japanese naturally excel in. Seek out the companies that are doing interesting and appealing business, regardless of the industry that they are in, or whether or not they are your competitors. Study them to see if there is anything you can learn. It will also be beneficial to study the companies that failed. There is always something you can learn from them too.

So far I have discussed mitori keiko as if it is only practiced by the Japanese, but actually there are masters of it outside Japan. One of these masters is the late Steve Jobs. When he visited the XEROX Palo Alto Research Center (PARC), he saw a graphical user interface (GUI) operated by a mouse, and then came up with the idea of attaching a mouse to a computer and made it a reality.

Steve Jobs was a genius in observing and adopting what he didn't know from another industry and product, and then incorporating it in his own product to create an innovative result.

Lladro's Hina Dolls match a modern space
and caused a new sensation.

THERE IS NO SUCH THING AS THE PERFECT SHOT

12

Perfectionism in organizations can keep them from gaining momentum.

WHY THE JAPANESE CAN'T SPEAK ENGLISH

Japan is a mysterious country. Educational standards and intelligence levels are both high, and yet there are many people who do not speak English. As I have learned more about this, I have found out that the Japanese can read simple English, but they are otherwise quite poor at listening to and speaking English.

Being an island nation, the Japanese have not had many opportunities to speak English and this may be a factor that has prevented them from improving their English language abilities.

However, I believe the main cause is the perfectionist nature of Japanese culture. The Japanese know the correct grammar to use and the vocabulary when reading and writing, but if they cannot form perfect sentences as they speak, they feel ashamed and therefore do not speak English. I feel they are stuck in this negative cycle.

Personally, I can express smoothly my ideas in Japanese; however, I am not as proficient as a native. I am often required to make speeches and I always wonder if I should speak French or English and get help from an interpreter, but I feel that I can communicate better if I speak Japanese myself. After giving a speech, I am always aware of the imperfect nature of my command of Japanese and feel remorse over it. But when I ask those around me if I sounded okay, they always tell me, "It was fine, Chouchan; it was great."

Nobody *expects* to hear perfect Japanese from me. Japanese people don't expect a French man to speak perfect Japanese.

This same principle applies to the Japanese as well. Nobody is expecting the Japanese to speak perfect English. It is *their own* expectation to speak perfect English. What they should do, in order to improve, is to speak English, regardless of their level of fluency, at every opportunity. Rather than spending time trying to master perfect English, it is far more important to find opportunities to use it. This struggle in the mind, between waiting to be 'perfect' in order to be ready to take a challenge, or tackling the challenge while still feeling insecure and 'imperfect', is something I have experienced in my journey to apply to the examinations in Kyudo. When you walk on the path of the examinations, it feels like you have to climb one mountain after the other. Each grade (dan) is a new challenge, as it presents new mental and technical difficulties. There is then the temptation to apply for a test only when you feel you have practised enough and are worthy of the level you are applying to. The problem with this thinking is that you may never feel ready and you will always find a reason to postpone your application. I fell into this trap after my 4th dan. After you pass the 4th dan, you are eligible to apply for the 5th dan after a period of six months. I did not feel sufficiently ready, so that my first attempt was only four years later. And finally, it took me 15 years to progress from the 4th dan to the 5th dan. As a lesson from this past approach, I decided to change my thinking and to apply to the tests regularly. In doing so, even if my shooting varies in quality, depending on my condition at the times of the test, the process of trying (and perhaps failing) has given me opportunities to learn and strengthen my shooting and understanding of Kyudo.

Whatever the challenge we face – be it in languages, business, or Kyudo – rather than waiting for the time to possess 'perfect' ability, it is far more important to find opportunities to express our ability of the moment and to learn from this.

PERFECTION IN BUSINESS IS AN ILLUSION OF THE MIND

In Kyudo, we aim for a perfect shot, but we also know that there is no such thing. This is the difference with modern Western archery, where a bull's-eye shot is perfect in itself. In Kyudo, we can always aim for a better form, and a purer spirit in our shooting. Knowing that our practice is an endless quest, we just keep making an effort, aiming for the ideal shot. This is the soul and spirit of Kyudo.

Equally, there is no such thing as perfection in business. It may be due to Japanese perfectionism that they have achieved a standard of high-quality products, not seen anywhere else in the world. It is because material things are never perfect that we keep on making an effort and aiming for the ideal. That is the fascinating part of business and Kyudo.

It is wonderful to seek excellence, but we should not forget about the pitfalls of perfectionism. Perfectionism in an organization is a big problem. You can aim for flawlessness to a point where you slow down and become stymied as a company and lose momentum.

Perfection can result in a culture where decisions are made only after several discussions, research upon research, and making sure that there are no flaws or problems. That is often how big corporate organizations execute changes. But by the time you devise a perfect plan that everyone feels secure about, more often than not it has lost its freshness and become stale and hackneyed.

For the Japanese it is particularly important to avoid this practice. As the Japanese market gradually shrinks (due to lower birth rates), this is making the potential for market growth rather difficult. It is becoming increasingly important to gain new customers by identifying their needs through trial and error, by working within a smaller market. Errors are often the very thing that help you find a new market.

In times where speed is a competitive advantage, the organizational perfectionism of not allowing mistakes and failures can be a serious hindrance. When you seek perfection, you are afraid of making the important mistakes which will help you to understand and move forward with business and projects. When you become overly concerned with perfection, it becomes difficult to start anything. This mindset will not generate anything new.

It is also important to disregard the mindset of not forging new paths or fresh initiatives until all the conditions are right. When you start a new business or a new project, you never have all the information you need and you never have a perfect infrastructure. So, you should start with what you can do with a small team and do it speedily. We are already in a time where it is no longer the case that the large always defeats the small: it is now the fast that beats the big.

The key to success for any new project is to move it forward, in small, incremental steps, moment by moment. As we say in Kyudo, through one shot at time we will gradually build our form. Shooting is an iterative process, where we learn from each shot, and shoot each new shot with a higher aspiration than the previous one. And one day, our shooting form looks like it has taken a big leap forward from where it was before. This learning and growing process is as relevant in archery as it is in business.

Rather than worrying about perfection, it is important to keep trying continuously, without agonizing about success or failure. As is said in Japan: "To continue is what builds strength."

THE MOMENT THE ARROW LEAVES THE BOW

13

The timing of a decision comes on the spot.
When deciding, decide boldly: on the spot.

THE TURNING POINT IN DECISION MAKING

What quality will help you to get a leadership role in a company? Is it passion, maturity, emotional intelligence, the ability to get things done or strategic vision? All of these traits are adjacent to a more essential quality, which is the strength and wisdom to make decisions on the spot and take responsibility for one's own decision. Whether you are a boss or a subordinate, people will respect you for your ability to make decisions at the proper time, without wavering.

Kyudo teaches about the importance and the quality of the moment. The entire outcome of the shooting is dependent on the instant of the release of the arrow. All prior movements culminate in the sudden discharge of the arrow. Though you could have trained your body and mind for many years, still the success or failure of your shot on the day of the exam will be manifested upon the suddenness of the release.

In the stage of 'kai' (full draw), there is no room for hesitation and/or procrastination. The arrow has to be released; it cannot be held forever. However, as explained previously, the proper timing cannot be planned and archers may fall in to the trap of two types of weakness:

1. 'Hayake'– releasing too soon. The archer releases the arrow immediately after holding the bow in full draw.
2. 'Motare'– releasing too late. The archer holds the bow for too long and misses the timed release; when the arrow is finally released, the momentum has been lost.

In these situations, those observing the performance of the archer can immediately see that the shooting is lacking sharpness and profoundness.

When in the stage of kai, doubt and hesitation can grow. The desire to hit the target and the fear of not doing so reach their maximum potential at this time. Distracting thoughts of self-willing and self-doubt have the opportunity to build up in this stage. But if you hesitate and start to confirm details of your technique to appease yourself, your mind stops your body from steadily growing to face the increasing force of the bow. Your whole shooting appears to be a succession of stop and start, lacking continuity, and in the very moment when you release the arrow, your body flexes, resulting in a poor and weak shot. This is the total opposite of ideal shot. In kai, my body and heart are supposed to extend endlessly. Throughout my years of training, I have been fighting with the struggles of the mind at the moment of kai.

This training has made me aware of the preciousness of moment in business. There is a Japanese saying, "Treasure every encounter, for it may be your last."

The states of 'hayake' and 'motare' can also be experienced in business and in making decisions. For example, hayake is when you rush to a decision without taking the time to get the required information and input from your team, and motare is when you look for certainty and consensus and procrastinate, whilst in the meantime missing the right timing for making a decision. Motare is frequent in large organizations, and the delay of the moment of decisions is a strong barrier to innovation.

MAKING CONSTANT DECISIONS

In Kyudo, once you are in the stage of full draw, you cannot put off shooting. The moment you hesitate, your shot will lose momentum. You should be daring to release the arrow, and if it doesn't hit the mark, then you can use that as an opportunity to learn from your mistakes. After each shot, the only concern should be regarding how to improve the next time. We need to keep shooting and aim to do it better than the last time.

In Kyudo, the release of the arrow is followed immediately by a hit or a miss, so it is a natural process to understand the importance of good and accurate timing. However, in the office, there is no such single moment of seeing the immediate effect of the decision. The effect – the fruit of the decision – happens in the market place a long time after the decision has been made. As a result of this cycle (decision and effect), managers put much more importance and priority on the *content* of the decision rather than on its timing, whereas in principle, when making a decision, you should be as critical regarding the timing as you are about the decision itself.

Also, note that you can make good and bad decisions, but if you make no decision because of fear of failure, then you will get no result. It is similar to a tree growing every day: you cannot see or feel the growth. After many years, though, you will be surprised to see how much it has grown. Repeatedly making small decisions will bear abundant fruit in the future. Moment upon moment, decisions are the engine to move a business forward.

So I always try to make a bold decision on the spot. Decisions made earlier will help the team move forward to the next step, and the business move forward too. If you miss the 'now', then the opportunity may be gone forever, as the market may have already moved to a new condition.

THE DECISION TO CHANGE JOBS

There is rarely a time when you have all the right conditions to make an important decision. When we reflect upon the decisions that we make in our life, this is often a dilemma that we have to solve.

I, myself, experienced a real struggle when I made the decision to change jobs. At the time, I was working for

LVMH Moët Hennessy Louis Vuitton, the global leading conglomerate of luxury brands. I was working at Hennessy as Business Development Director. In those days, I lived in France, and had a happy personal life. But I was not very satisfied with my business life. My role put me between the French and Japanese teams. I had to undertake a lot of trips and tackle opposing arguments from both sides. It was exhausting, both physically and mentally.

Then I received an offer to work as president for Lladro Japan, based in Tokyo. I asked some of my friends for advice, and they all said, "You are working for the worldwide leader of luxury brands. Why would you change jobs and work for the Japanese branch of a Spanish company?"

I hesitated: if I were to serve as a president for this Spanish company, what would my future be after that? If I were to change jobs, I would need to leave France, and my children would have to change schools to a French school in Japan. Would they be able to adjust to the new environment? All these thoughts kept me from making a decision.

Around that time, my wife said to me, "The question is not about where you live or which company you work for. It is about what type of work you do. Shouldn't that be the sole criteria for your decision?"

These words helped me to find an answer. This was the first time in my career that I had the opportunity to be fully in charge of the P&L of a company.

I focused my thinking on this single criteria of the content of the job and the why behind it. My logical mind was at peace. Then as the next step, I needed the will power and energy to simply decide and move forward. I remembered what my Kyudo teacher told me when I had a poor release with my body slackening at the critical point: "Stretch your body decisively, without mentally stopping and without worrying where the arrow will go."

That is exactly what I did: I put all my energy behind the single criteria of the decision. And I moved resolutely forward to change jobs.

Working at Lladro Japan was very fulfilling. Seeing my accomplishments there, someone invited me to come to work for Godiva Japan. These years at Godiva Japan have also been very exciting.

The fear of the unknown is what prevents us from making difficult decisions. However, unless we make a bold decision without vacillating, a new world will not open up to us.

MANAGING IN THE DIGITAL AGE

The present age is unique, in the sense that time and innovation have never moved so fast at any point in history. This unstoppable acceleration was anticipated more than 70 years ago, in the seminal book of Rene Guenon, *The Reign of Quantity and the signs of Times*. This acceleration will go faster as technology continues to move us forward. We can sense the effects in our daily life and our companies, where mobile phones, the internet, and emails have changed our perception of the duration of time, be it day or year. This is the reign of the ephemeral: a picture on Snapchat and a message on twitter are forgotten in seconds.

On the contrary, practicing Kyudo in a dojo is akin to entering another world: one that has been transmitted from 1,000 years ago, and where time seems to have stopped. When you practice Kyudo or look at a Kyudo demonstration, the concentration of the archers, the rhythms of the movements, and the silence during the shooting, are transforming the value of the instant. It is as if the instant is reaching the timeless and the universal. In the stage of the full draw (kai), at the moment of maximum tension, there is neither past, nor future, there is only the 'now'.

What can Kyudo teach us for the business of our times? The digital age is exerting pressure as things change so fast, and we sometimes feel like we are drowning in a violent tornado of information and events. On the other hand, as in Kyudo, it gives us the opportunity in the corporate world to rediscover the importance of the instant. This may have implications not only in our day to day behaviour, but also in our strategic planning and marketing. The three- or five-year plan that we used to undertake should be viewed merely as a direction and aspiration and no longer as a firm path and commitment. The analysis of the past is no longer a guide for the future. Implementing this mindset change in our companies would force us to allocate fewer resources to the analysis and reporting of the past and more on creating the future.

The manager of our times should focus his discernment and decisions on the 'now', as the Kyudo archer does during his shooting.

BUSINESS ORIGINATING IN JAPAN IS THE BUSINESS OF THE FUTURE

14

The uniqueness of Japan is an inspiration for business in the age of globalization.

CONSUMERS IN JAPAN ARE THE MOST EXPERIENCED SHOPPERS IN THE WORLD

In the 1970s, Japanese manufacturers were very good at producing high-quality products at a low cost, and they captured the spotlight worldwide. Electronics companies such as Sony, Panasonic, and Sharp, in particular, claimed significant shares in many countries around the world, including America.

But in recent years, with China and Korea entering the market, Japan is losing its foothold. Given this shift, my view is that Japan should now compete by focusing on high-quality 'made-in-Japan' products, which Japan can be proud of, and should commit to uncompromising design and technological capability, rather than seeking the advantages of low-cost products.

Japanese companies should compete in the world market with a global vision right from the beginning, instead of selling their products first in Japan and exporting them, as they have up until now. Every year, tourists travel to Japan: one common reason for their visits is to purchase high-quality Japanese products at reasonable prices. Carefully designed household goods such as kitchen tools, drugs, sanitary goods, toilet seats with a warm-water bidet feature – as well as home electronic appliances – are all popular items among tourists, especially tourists from Asia. Since we are in the age of globalization, it is not only Japanese products that have the opportunity to be known worldwide, but also the Japanese brands built on these products.

There is another factor to which we should give attention from a worldwide perspective. That is the Japanese consumer. They have been brought up in a culture that historically has always had a keen sense for quality, craftsmanship and beauty. Modern Japanese consumers are refined, and have a great deal of experience in shopping. In the last 40 years, with the evolution of the Japanese economy, consumers have experienced all the stages in shopping, ranging from commodity goods at a low price to status items with high prices. In the last ten years, most the population has acquired a very discerning taste for all kind of product categories from all over the world. They have a keen eye for the products, and seek perfection in not only functional quality, but also in design, wrapping, advertisement and customer service. Even on a world-wide scale, Japanese consumers are very special.

Generally speaking, American consumers seek a good value proposition, while European consumers find value in life experiences rather than in material possessions. China is an emerging economic power, and Chinese consumers have less experience with products, when compared to Japanese consumers.

Many of the products and services that have been sifted through the strict standard of the Japanese market go well beyond the global standard. That is why so many inbound visitors come to the Tokyo districts of Ginza and Akihabara to purchase Japanese products. Products that have been tried and proven in Japan have won the trust of consumers around the world.

The Japanese people are also great at accepting and enjoying new things. It was Japanese consumers who first used the Walkman, a forerunner of the iPod, and took music on the go. The Japanese market has the power to accept the new and to push it into the wider world.

THINK LOCAL, SCALE GLOBAL

In 1972, when Godiva first launched its products in the Japanese market, they were selling imported products from Belgium, but things changed slowly over the years. For example, Godiva Japan took the lead in planning and designing Godiva's products for Valentine's Day, White Day, and other seasons. Some collections were then developed and produced in Japan and sold across the world – Europe, the US, and in Asia.

In fact, unlike in Europe and the US, the custom was of women giving men chocolate on Valentine's Day, and then men giving women chocolate on White Day. The Japanese specific way of celebrating this holiday is unique to the market, and the Japanese chocolate makers and consumers have enjoyed this custom for some time.

In the area of ice cream sales, Godiva Japan has been selling soft serve since 2013. It was sold only in Japan. Soft serve is generally fairly cheap and mainstream, while Godiva is an expensive chocolate brand. However, nobody had thought of linking these two factors.

But then some Japanese staff suggested, "Maybe we can serve somewhat luxurious soft serve that adults can enjoy." It was an interesting idea, so we proposed it to the Godiva headquarters, to which they replied that it would be fine to go ahead and start to sell soft serve in Japan only. Godiva is a company that respects region-specific initiatives and new development of relevant products in those regions.

We began by only releasing the soft serve product in a limited number of stores; however, it took off quickly, gaining popularity. Seeing that it was selling more than expected, I decided to sell it in Korea, where I was also in charge. In Korea, it attracted attention because this Godiva soft serve was the first premium soft serve in the market, and it became a hit. We then sold it in China, and it was a game changer for our business there. It attracted young customers and families to our brand and stores. Observing how it was a big hit in Asian countries, Godiva in America and Europe decided to sell soft serve as well. What originated in Japan was recognized as a global item. Other products originating in Japan, such as sables chocolate and cookies, were also launched in other markets around the world.

This phenomenon of innovation generated by a local business unit within a global organization has generated the interest of Harvard Business School, who came to interview Godiva Japan. They wrote a business case for MBA around the topic of globalization, which captured the essence of what we were doing. It was published in January 2017 under the title "Godiva Japan: Think Local, Scale Global."

Globalization is taking place within the food industry. The first wave has been observed with fast food chains and drinks, but there is still a tremendous potential for quality and premium foods to unlock. There are some challenges, as food is strongly related to local cultures and tastes. The factor of success will be how to blend the local relevancy of the ingredients with the globalization of a sophisticated taste, initiated by the craftsmanship of chefs.

In 2013, Washoku (traditional Japanese cuisine) was added to the UNESCO intangible heritage list. It shows the high level of Japanese chefs and the high quality of food and ingredients. But in the food industry there are no world-famous Japanese manufacturers like there are in the automobile and home appliance makers. Considering the high level of Washoku, Japanese food manufacturers have a lot of room for growth and they should eye the global market as they develop new products.

FROM THE JAPANESE SPIRIT TO GLOBAL ECONOMIC DEVELOPMENT

Japan is probably the country that has transformed itself from a feudal society to a developed economic society in the shortest period of time. The modernization of Japan dates from the Meiji era (1868-1912) and accelerated from the 1950s after the war. In the 1980s, Japan's GNP ranked second in the world, and it is now ranked as the 3rd economy in the world, after United States and China.

Rather than natural resources and the size of its domestic market, the primary asset of Japan is its people and the values they follow.

Even in the rush to modernization and the adoption of a Western style of economy, the values of the Japanese spirit have been preserved. This is due mainly to a profound respect for tradition, which is passed on from generation to generation. Also, the geographic position of Japan as an island has contributed to its unity of belief.

In his book *Bushido (the Way of the Samurai): the Soul of Japan*, Nitobe Inazo wrote that, even though the lifestyle of the Samurai had disappeared, the Japanese are still permeated by the ideals of their traditional virtues: rectitude, courage, benevolence, politeness, sincerity, honour, loyalty and self-control.

In the study of martial arts such as Kyudo, these virtues are an integral part of the practice. These virtues are also conductive to better management of companies. In a research paper about leadership, published in July 2005 in the *Harvard Business Review*, Jim Collins concluded that the best leaders in the long term (which he called 'level 5 leaders') are the ones who can embody this paradox of having both "humility and fierce resolve". This combination of humility and strong determination reminds me of the senior Japanese archers who try repeatedly to pass and fail a Kyudo test at a very high level (from 6th dan onwards): they never cease repeatedly trying, and at the same time, when they fail they recognize humbly their deficiencies.

In addition to its sincere and diligent people, Japan has two other economic assets:

1. A market comprised of the most refined consumers in the world.
2. Products and services that are continuously improved through the screening of those consumers.

I believe that, owing to these two areas, which are still not yet very well known worldwide, business originating from Japan will attract attention.

In addition, I think that we are entering an age where more and more of Japan's capable businessmen can work overseas to bring their skills to a multicultural team as part of a global organization.

In Asia, Japan is already the trendsetter for the consumer developments for the whole region. Business people from China, Korea and ASEAN countries regularly visit Japan to look for new product ideas and business models to bring back to their own countries. Japan is ahead of the curve in the cycle of consumption of products and services.

Some multinationals focus their efforts on China and, in this process, overlook the potential of Japan as a business intelligence centre that can elaborate and guide a successful strategy for the whole Asian region.

Japan has all the unique assets to become a centre of business knowledge and innovation that brings its positive influence to the global scene.

THE JAPANESE MARKET MOVES WITH THE SEASONS

15

In harmony with nature: seasonal or time-limited products have value all on their own.

JAPANESE MARKETING THAT CREATES
A REASON FOR PURCHASE

Japan has four beautiful seasons. We have seen earlier how nature (shizen) has influenced the traditional arts of Japan, in the sense that the performance of the artist tries to imitate how nature operates.

This closeness to nature in the art of Kyudo is also expressed in the equipment you use: Experienced archers generally employ equipment that is made with natural elements and by the hands of qualified craftsmen: the bow and arrows are made in bamboo, the bow string is made from hemp, and the glove is handmade from leather. In comparison, modern Western archery has developed a compound bow and a string with Dacron fabric. In a modern world, where technology and machines are increasingly predominant, the link with nature is a peaceful influence that helps you to centre yourself. It also helps you to be aware of the harmony between the individual and the universe, or as the ancient Greeks would say, the microcosm and the macrocosm.

Nature has also deeply influenced the daily life of the Japanese people. Having lived in Japan for years, I am always amazed how the Japanese show a deep respect for nature and value living in harmony with nature. Even when you live in such a big metropolis as Tokyo, you can sense this intention. In each of the four seasons, they have developed and cherished many customs. They enjoy seasonal events such as Shogatsu (New Year's Holiday), Setsubun (the day before the beginning of spring), Hina-matsuri (the Hina doll festival), Hachiju-hachi-ya (the eighty-eighth day after the beginning of spring), Tango no Sekku (the Boys' Festival), Tanabata (the star festival), Chushu-no-Meigetsu (the harvest moon), Toji (winter solstice), Omisoka (New Year's Eve) and many more.

As you walk about the various towns in Japan, you will notice that they change their window displays with the seasons.

Packaging and wrapping also strongly reflect the seasons. The cultural sense of seasons and customs are part of the driving force that runs the economy.

From my experience at Lladro, I learned that the Japanese like seasonal limited-time offers. When selling seasonal products, one of the crucial factors for making them a big hit is by decorating the shop's window displays according to the season and using seasonal colours for packaging.

At Godiva, we make annual plans, and create limited edition products by changing the taste and the colour of packaging according to the season. When we started selling autumn specials, we used dark brown packaging, which reminds customers of the leaves changing colours, and this proved to be a big hit. This type of seasonal colour coordination was born out of the unique Japanese aesthetic sense. Indeed, the service of carefully and beautifully wrapping presents is unique to Japan. No other country has this custom of altering wrapping paper depending on the season. And attaching a sheet of paper on a gift box that has writing such as 'oiwai' (congratulations) or 'oseibo' (the end of the year gift), is a very sensible custom, unique to Japan.

The Japanese are very particular about 'shun' (specialty of the season) and 'hatsumono' (first fish, fruit, or vegetable of the season) and people are keen to obtain seasonal ingredients such as 'takenoko' (bamboo shoots), 'shinmai' (new crop rice), 'hatsu-gatsuo' (first bonito flakes of the season) 'sanma' (first saury of the season), 'matsutake' (mushrooms), and 'tai' (sea bream). The Japanese don't hesitate to spend money when it comes to products like this. Seasonal food encourages more consumption. It is valuable because you can eat it only during a certain season.

The ideas of shun and hatsumono give people a reason to buy and eat something immediately, rather than at other times of the year. The custom of eating 'unagi' (eel) on Doyono-ushi-no-hi (day of the ox) also gives people a reason for buying and eating eel immediately on this day. There are other customs relevant to the seasons: sakura (cherry blossoms), are also important to Japan. 'Hanami', the act of flower viewing, is a very special and enjoyable event. The sight of so many Japanese people gathering beneath sakura trees and having a picnic with friends and family is quite amazing.

Sakura bloom for a short period once a year. The transient beauty is a symbol of the impermanence of life and makes it very precious. This gave me an idea, while I was working for Lladro, to offer a 'sakura series' every spring. The theme was a beautiful woman under a sakura tree, and it was very well received. We also launched delicious Godiva cookies inspired by the sakura theme.

Two other seasonal customs that drew my attention were 'ochugen', summer gifts, and 'oseibo', end-of-year gifts. This custom is also very unique to Japan. Giving a gift to express your gratitude twice a year is a wonderful tradition – there are few other countries that have such a beautiful custom.

However, in recent years, more and more urban Japanese under the age of 50 have stopped practicing this custom, feeling that it is just an empty formality. The problem is that it has lost its original meaning, and evolved into a burdensome obligation. Initially, this tradition was influenced by Confucianism, where the respect (rei) to others implies social interactions that are built on the values of harmony and hierarchy of the society. As I practice Kyudo, I was sensitive to the importance of formalized actions based on rei, and how they are helpful in expressing gratitude (kansha) to others. Ochugen and oseibo are traditions that should be revitalized by bringing back the meaning they convey.

I think it is a very unique Japanese marketing strategy that blends the uniqueness of the seasons with consumer desire. The example of how Japan can implement nature into everyday urban life can be a source of inspiration to other businesses in other countries.

GODIVA'S NEW WHITE DAY: A VALENTINE'S DAY FROM A MAN'S PERSPECTIVE

In Japan, after Valentine's Day in February, there is the custom of White Day, which is 14 March, exactly one month after Valentine's Day. White Day is a unique Japanese gift occasion when men are supposed to reciprocate gifts to the women that gave them chocolates on Valentine's Day.

At Godiva, we conducted a survey on this gift season, and found that Japanese men do not really enjoy it. It became a duty to give something in return for what you received on Valentine's Day. However, I realized that we could make White Day the day when men give gifts to those they like, those they love, or to say simply 'thank you', regardless of whether or not they received chocolate from that person on Valentine's Day. This, I believed, would make White Day more exciting.

When I first made this suggestion, some women said, "I would hesitate to receive chocolate from a man I didn't give any chocolate to." But what I had in mind was to make it a happy day when men willingly express their feelings of thankfulness. Just giving a gift in return is not especially spontaneous, is it? Maybe Japanese men could be more active in approaching women. Japanese men are not very good at expressing their feelings. Perhaps because I am French, I feel that Japanese men should express their feelings more freely.

Since 2015, Godiva Japan has launched the campaign 'New White Day' where we encourage giving gifts of your own free will. This new concept of White Day has not spread yet, but young men supported us and our sales have grown.

PART 3

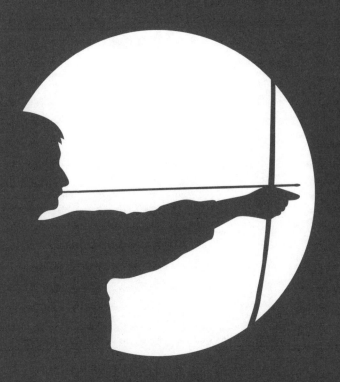

HOW TO MAKE YOUR WORK MEANINGFUL AND ENJOYABLE

THE RIGHT INNER INTENTION

16

Employees should be able to find joy in their work. Praise employees to help them flourish. The strong enterprises are those that cultivate people.

THE COMPANY'S MISSION FOR ITS EMPLOYEES

In work, in hobbies, and in life, knowing why we are doing what we are doing is very important. The answer to this 'why' is what we call 'our mission'.

Let me give you an example. In Kyudo there is a saying, 'The bow builds the man'. The great mission of Kyudo is not to hit the target or to get better at shooting, but to perfect the human nature as you learn to shoot an arrow. And this mission is what provides deep meaning and joy to the art of Kyudo.

It is the same with work: if the company has a meaningful mission and you are in agreement with their values and purpose, then you can feel joy in the work you do. I became convinced of this at the time of the Great East Japan Earthquake in 2011. The earthquake and tsunami devastated a wide area, causing a nuclear accident that brought about a power supply shortage. There was plenty of confusion at that time. It was an extremely difficult and tough time for Japan. Most of the luxurious brands from overseas decided to close until things had stabilized, but at Godiva we decided to continue with business as usual: when customers went out shopping for a little ease and normality during this difficult time, we believed it would be dispiriting to have our shops closed.

Our staff at the stores received gracious comments from many customers: "I went to Godiva's shop and bought some chocolate and got to experience some happiness for a time, enjoying delicious chocolate. During this time of crisis, it cheered me up a bit."

A little thing like selling chocolate provided a little bit of happiness to the Japanese people. Godiva's mission is, as I have said repeatedly, to spread happiness through offering chocolate. We are filled with deep joy as we fulfil this mission.

At the Kyudo practice hall, we often recite Li Ki shagi in unison, which is excerpts on archery from the ancient Chinese Confucian classic 'Li Ki', the Book of Rites. And in this Li Ki shagi is the following quote:

"After having acquired the proper inner intention and correctness in outward appearance, the bow and arrow can be handled resolutely."

This teaching means that, in order to shoot accordingly and hit the target, the inner man and the outer man should be in complete harmony. You must first of all have your inner intention right, straighten out your outward appearance, and treat the bow and arrow with care.

Applying this to a company means that in order to make those outside the company – the customers – happy, you should try to make sure that the workplace is a happy environment and that the workers are happy too. Kyudo taught me the importance of searching for the harmony between things within the company (the inner world) and things outside the company (the outer world).

CUSTOM OF CELEBRATING EMPLOYEES' SUCCESSES

Godiva's Headquarters are located in New York City in the US, and they have a custom of celebrating the success of the staff worldwide. Godiva Japan has received Global Awards twice from the Headquarters for producing outstanding results. We at Godiva Japan also give awards to the employees who make excellent contributions. Traditionally, Japanese bosses often make comments when they want to point out mistakes and give corrections, but tend to stay quiet when their subordinates do well.

My Kyudo teacher, Hiroko Uragami, has the 'Hanshi' title. This is someone who has been recognized as exemplifying the highest degree of conduct, dignity, and perfection of ability, together with the highest quality of discernment. She is the first woman to obtain 10th dan, and is an excellent performer. You could call her a master of Kyudo.

Ms Uragami never told her students that they were no good. She would quietly watch us shoot, and give us praise when she found something good, and then add, "If you did it this way, it would be even better." Even when my shooting was so poor, she simply smiled or laughed out loud and watched over me. Her merciful look helped me a great deal more than stern words of correction, and it gave me a positive outlook. It is because of her and her style of teaching that I have been able to continue Kyudo all this time.

It's important to find good qualities in people and to help them grow through encouragement. The days of creating the same type of people by scolding are over.

MAKE HAPPY. BE HAPPY.

My ideal company is a group of professionals with diverse personalities, where each of them grows to their full potential through adequate tasks and responsibilities. This group would be able to handle any situation efficiently and with respect for each individual. And as result of this right framework, the company would deliver superior performance. It does not make sense to have someone who loves making chocolate undertake sales, or for someone who likes selling to do desk work. Employees should utilize their strengths and enjoy what they do. To make the best of their skills and cultivate them further is important for the future of companies and societies.

In the 80s, top universities taught their MBA students that people are a variable resource, like any other resources in the company. Nowadays, MBA students are taught that engagement of employees has a direct link with the company's performance, and that individual development plans should be carefully crafted. For companies, it should be a top priority to cultivate workers who can express their talents through their job and, as a result, lead the business in a good direction.

As I said previously, there is a saying in Kyudo, "The bow builds the man." The great mission of Kyudo is to cultivate people through training and practice. The mission of all businesses should also be to cultivate people.

In retail companies, many of us have difficulties in retaining store staff. At Godiva Japan, our staff turnover is much lower than the retail average in the market. I believe this is due to our staff loving their jobs. We encourage this passion for the job by giving constant training that enables retail staff to learn how to perform better in their duties and feel more fulfilled. We have different types of training sessions that we hold 170 times during the year, such as:

- Concierge Training Course: gain a deeper understanding of the principles of Godiva's service; gain expertise in customer service through practical training.
- Image Enhancement Training: learn make-up techniques, behaviourism, and other necessary information required of a retail professional.
- Role Play: practical training with chocolates in various scenarios.
- Orientation (at company headquarters): Receive an explanation about each department, the role they play, and the content of their work.
- Communication & Coaching Training: receive the training necessary to cultivate and provide feedback to the team working in the store.

When I see how Japanese staff put their heart into this practice, their focus reminds me of the sincerity and diligence of archers practicing in the dojo.

In the shopping malls where Godiva shops are located, there are competitions among all the shops, focusing on customer service skills; Godiva staff often compete for customer goodwill and have been doing well in these competitions.

In a training exercise, I remember that one excellent staff member lost in the final match, and thus didn't become the 'champion' in the training. The reason for her loss was that she took longer than the allotted time. It would have been perfect if she had been able to help the customer check out at the register and bid them farewell, but the time was up before she took the customer to the register. She was shedding tears of disappointment, but I said to her, "It took longer because you were taking the time to serve the customer with care. Thank you for showing them the high quality of Godiva's customer service!" In real life, I believe the customer would have been satisfied. I was very proud of her for doing such a good job in serving the customer.

CREATING A STRONG ORGANIZATION ORIGINATES FROM A HAPPY WORKING ENVIRONMENT

In Godiva, we are all inspired by the motto of our parent company Yildiz Holding, which is: 'Make Happy. Be Happy'. Every year, on the third Thursday of November, we celebrate 'Make Happy, Be Happy Day' and invite the families and children of our staff to our offices. This day honours the memory of Sabri Ülker, founder of Yildiz Holding, who believed that, "No matter where in the world you live, you have the right to a happy childhood." I really love the atmosphere full of laughter and joyful energy in the office on this special day.

In truly strong organizations, people work not because they are told to, but because they want to. If you feel your work life is boring, you are probably keeping your job mainly for its salary. You are experiencing a conflict between the inner man and the outer man. Our ideal in the workplace should be higher. As it is told in *The Bible* (Matthew 4:4): "Man shall not live on bread alone."

The pursuit of having happy consumers and employees is an endless effort similar to the pursuit of the ideal shot in Kyudo. This quest is what makes our work and career meaningful and fulfilling.

Make Happy. Be Happy.

THE IMPORTANT THINGS ARE SENSED

17

Create the environment and the time
to master principles through
personal experience.

LEARN CORPORATE PHILOSOPHY
BY PERSONAL EXPERIENCE

In Kyudo there is a saying, "The bow is understood through personal experience." What is meant by personal experience is that the understanding should be with the whole being. It is said that in your practice there are three levels of knowledge.

The first level is with your mind; this is where you understand what has to be done: for example, bring your elbow lower for the drawing of the bow, grasp the bow like a baby's hand without excessive tension, etc. This theoretical knowledge is a necessary step, but it is of no avail if you cannot make it yours with your own body during the shooting. I was myself amazed to realize that what I thought I understood could not be embodied in my shooting, despite the fact that I tried very hard.

The second level is with your body when it reaches some understanding and can perform from time to time the shape that the mind had asked of it. In this stage, you get some glimpses of understanding but this is not yet stabilized in your body, as your shooting is still irregular.

The third level, which is called 'Chi' (knowledge), is when the mind and the body work regularly in harmony, and because of the stability of the shooting, the desired form is yours. This level can be achieved only through intensive practice and repetition of the same movements, going through trial and error. All students of Kyudo and other martial arts go through this learning process, its difficulty, and the required intensive practice to be able to embody regularly what the mind has understood.

The metaphor of the archer tells us what kind of obstacles we may face in the workplace when we want to implement a corporate philosophy in the company. The company is an organization that has a body, much like the body of the archer. No presentations, words, or posters on the walls alone will be enough to bring the corporate philosophy to life in the body of the organization. These first steps are necessary to obtain theoretical knowledge, but, as for the archer, practice – or, to use corporate language, training – is a must for the company's philosophy to take shape in the organization.

The most successful types of training are the ones that engage the staff beyond their rational mind. To lead and facilitate this training we asked an executive coach, Philippe Grall, president of the company Equilibre, to elaborate programs on how Godiva staff could experience these values with their whole being.

Godiva has a global mission to spread joy and happiness around the world through chocolates and a vision to be "the world's most iconic premium chocolate company". In line with these values, we recruit people who have these five traits: they must be purposeful, positive, collaborative, agile, and resilient.

When we did a training course on the Vision, we asked the staff how they would see the company in five years. But rather than asking them to think individually and write their thoughts on post them on a board, we asked different teams to design their own Vision on a big sheet of paper. All of us suddenly had to act in a different way to the roles that we normally played in the office. We had to design images with colour pens! This process was fun and engaging, and the result was inspiring for our future (cf. figure A). All the designs of the Vision from the different teams were then assembled in a booklet that was distributed to all employees.

We also undertook some other training exercises to develop proper traits and values in the company.

The way to engage people was this time to ask them to imagine a business meeting scene and play the role where one of the staff would successfully embody the desired behaviour while the other would perform the opposite role. For example, for collaborative behaviour, transparency is a key element. So the staff played a scene, where one was collaborative and transparent while discussing some business agenda with someone who was the opposite. We took videos of these role-plays and it was amazing to see how staff were so engaged in their appointed roles. We then got feedback that, aside from their evident enjoyment, this approach made them understand at a deeper level what the desired behaviours meant.

Training for the corporate environment is the same as in practice for martial arts: the critical factors are repetition and content to bring forth the form in the body of the organization. When training activation reaches a certain level, we can see that staff naturally exhibit the desired behaviours in their daily actions. But even at this stage, regular training is necessary to prevent different habits or behaviours from overcoming the desirable actions. As it is said in martial arts, bad habits spread like weeds, so we should constantly polish ourselves. It is also critical that top management figures train themselves in order to set the proper example to the organization. The leadership team of the company is the spirit of the organization. Its influence permeates the whole body of the organization, in the same way that the archer directs his mind and vital energy to his whole body to perform a proper shooting. Japanese proverbs, such as "fish start to perish by the head", are often quoted to describe the responsibility of the top management for sustaining a healthy organization.

Japanese traditional arts such as Kyudo may appear very simple, as their movements are limited and always the same. They may look easy, but there is tremendous depth and complexity beneath the surface, so that people keep practicing for life, and still make new discoveries along the way. Simplicity is deceptive, as an art form may seem very easy to understand through the mind, but extremely difficult to implement in terms of action. Corporate philosophy and values should always be simple: they must be self-explanatory and easily understood by everyone; despite this apparent simplicity, only very few companies are truly able to make their philosophies relevant and practicable on a day-to-day basis among their staff.

Designs of the Vision of the future of Godiva Japan,
as conceived by two different teams of employees.

A 'SECOND LIFE'

18

A New Life. What should be done now in order to live a fulfilling 'second life'?

PRACTICING WORK-LIFE BALANCE

The expression 'work-life balance' is relatively new; it was first coined in the UK in the late 1970s and it has been utilized in the corporate world in the last 20 years or so. It describes the healthy balance between an individual's work and their personal commitments, such as their leisure activities, their family and private life. The very existence of this term 'work-life balance' itself is a symptom of an anomaly in the life of the modern man, as it alludes to an imbalance between work and life. It is as if work and life were acting as two opposing forces, in which work must be detrimental to a balanced and healthy life. With the fast pace of globalization, the increasing demands that companies place upon employees has indeed created a life imbalance, which has generated a source of tremendous stress for many individuals. In addition, it has been documented that this phenomenon has resulted in detrimental performance for the company.

In Kyudo, it is fundamental that the left and right arm work in balance to draw the bow and then release the arrow with the hands moving equally in a straight line to the left and the right. To teach this technique, masters communicate a metaphor that has been transmitted throughout the times: 'The left arm is the husband and the right arm is the wife. The husband and wife must perform their respective roles in proper harmony, so that the children grow in a straight way, as the arrow flying straight to its target.' Applying the metaphor of Kyudo to the workplace, it can be said that these two forces between work and life should complement each other harmoniously, just as the left and right arm do in Japanese archery. In so doing, we can expect the individual to lead a fulfilling life, grow into their full potential and perform better at work.

Today, work-life balance is still an issue for many companies. At Godiva Japan, we support our employees in having a good work-life balance, and they are very grateful for this. For example, Fridays are called 'Happy Fridays': after two o'clock, the employees go out and visit our shops or do something fulfilling for their personal life. Through this practice, we encourage them to feel and experience the importance of activities outside the office. As we are in the business of providing happiness, this is a beneficial practice for both the individual and the company. It is often by walking around in town that new ideas and services for the consumer can pop up. Unfortunately, this type of thinking is not very common in today's business world. Leisure and hobbies tend to not be pursued as much as work, and they are not recognized with the same regard and high esteem as career success. Many people only truly start considering activities outside their work, such as hobbies, as they approach the retirement age. But it is often too late to start thinking about it then, as the physical limitations of age may constrain certain activities.

"What to do with the second half of one's life?" asked Peter Drucker. Forty years ago, in his book *Management, Tasks and Responsibilities*, he explained, "A manager has to be able to develop a life of his own, and outside the organization before he is in his mid-forties. He needs this for himself, but he needs it also for the organization. For the manager who, at age forty-five, retires on the job because he has no more interest in life, is not likely to make any further contribution to the business. He owes it to himself – and to the business – to develop himself as a person."

Many people only have vague ideas about their second life, such as, "I will be able to take it easy after I retire," or, "I want to do some menial work in a small subsidiary company." Perhaps many believe this to be left-over time and treat it with an unhealthy disregard.

This question is particularly pertinent for Japanese society, as it has become the most aged – and long-lived – society in the world, with more than one quarter of its population aged over 65. If Japan succeeds in bringing creative answers to this issue, it can also set examples of solutions for other rapidly aging societies such as the US, the UK, China, Korea and Hong Kong.

MAKING THE BEST OF YOUR CALLING IN LIFE

When I started Kyudo at the age of 29, it was intended to be a solitary pursuit. I did not even inform my friends that I had started this discipline. I had never practised any martial art, or even seen a demonstration of Kyudo. I was attracted to this Eastern path of self-development because one single word strongly resonated in me: 'target'. Target as the symbol of the desire that you want to satisfy or to subdue. This was my private inner journey. An oasis of freedom in the modern world of achievements and commitments. It was disconnected from the demands and the constraints of society. I was just practising regularly, week after week. My practice of shooting at targets in archery started to slowly impact upon my practice of management aiming at business targets. And one day, I received a totally unexpected call. It was from the Secretary General of the Kyudo Federation, and he informed me that I had been nominated as a Board Director of the International Federation. I was appointed to help the Federation in its process of internationalization. I was also asked to assist the Japanese Federation in making Kyudo more relevant to the general public in Japan. What had started as personal quest was now bringing me to take a public role. What began as the influence of Kyudo upon business was now becoming the influence of business upon Kyudo: the Kyudo federation had called me in order to benefit from my experience in management.

My experience of business and organizations naturally gave me a new perspective on the world of Kyudo for traditional Japanese organizations. When I started to look at Kyudo in the same way I was looking at brands, I realized that Kyudo faces very interesting challenges and a large potential market.

First of all, everyone in Japan knows what Kyudo is and they are very proud of its long history. However, it has an issue of apparent irrelevancy in comparison with other martial arts, such as Judo and Kendo, which have ten times more practitioners than Kyudo. To increase its members further, Kyudo would need to formulate a strategy by:

1. Revitalizing the brand image of Kyudo. It is perceived as a traditional and austere martial art. In business, we would say, "It is not a brand for me." The authentic tradition of Kyudo should be carefully preserved and it should be communicated and taught in a relevant way to target the population of today's modern times.
2. Making Kyudo relevant to people's lifestyle. The occasions and places to practise are often unknown and not easily accessible from home or work. The places and available times of practices should be expanded into schools, universities, sports clubs, and company-related activities, with a focus on the benefits to individuals' mindsets.

The traditional arts, such as Kyudo, transmit a message that is vital for our modern society to comprehend. Today's unprecedented wave of change and turbulence requires authentic teachings that originated centuries ago, to help bring perspective and stability. However, throughout this process of growth, it is critical to stay true to the essence and tradition of the art. The example of the internationalization of Judo has shown that, while it has gained tremendous recognition internationally, it has at the same time adapted too much to some Western demands, and has lost of some its traditional Japanese values.

The Kyudo Federation is a non-profit organization and currently managed by a chairman and a board of directors, which mainly comprises Masters archers. While this ensures that the archery tradition is transmitted without discontinuity, it also prevents the development of the organization, as Master archers are generally not people experienced in the management of an organization.

In a future stage of the organizational development of the Kyudo Federation, we could envision that the teaching of Kyudo itself would be under the sole authority of the Master archers, as it is nowadays, while on the other hand, the executive tasks of the organization could be delegated to professional managers.

I believe that cultural activities, when seen through the eye of an executive, can unlock new perspectives and potential developments. The Kyudo Federation regroups all the forms of traditional archery, and has the mission of promoting the essence and practice of the martial art of Japanese archery to the general public, in Japan and around the world. This openly-shared goal is a recent change. In the past, the teachings of Kyudo were secretly guarded by the different traditional schools of archery. It was even thought that the teaching and the art should not be communicated outside the selected disciples of the teacher.

In July 2014, the International Kyudo Federation was scheduled to hold the second Kyudo World Cup in Paris. I realized that the Kyudo World Cup was not yet publicized in Japan. From my business perspective, I could not help but think, 'It would be a shame to go unnoticed when we hold this World Cup in France. It would draw more attention if we undertook more PR activities.'

Thus, I decided to write to Christian Masset, the then French ambassador to Japan. In the letter, I explained that the second Kyudo World Cup would be held in Paris, and that France had won the first prize in the First World Cup, but that this World Cup was virtually unknown globally, so we would like to undertake PR activities; I asked for his help and support, as France would be the host country.

I soon received a reply from the ambassador, asking me to come to the French Embassy. When I went to talk to him, Ambassador Masset promised to give us his full support by holding a press conference at the French Embassy for the International Kyudo Federation and inviting the countries participating in the World Cup, as well as the press. Moreover, an inauguration ceremony was scheduled for the same time at the French Embassy, followed by a Kyudo demonstration and a party.

On the day of the event, in the beautiful garden of the French Embassy, Takeo Ishikawa, Hanshi (Master) 9th dan, the President of International Kyudo Federation, did 'sharei' (ceremonial shooting) and some high school students did 'shukusha' (shooting for celebration). Her Imperial Highness Princess Takamado, Honorary President of the International Kyudo Federation, along with ambassadors from different countries, politicians, and many others attended the event; the party was a big success. The International Kyudo Federation had never been afforded this type of opportunity, and it created very positive international PR opportunities for Kyudo.

Traditional arts and business can interact with each other for the merit of the individual and society. For the individual businessperson, this provides a source of knowledge and a task to perform in the later part of life. For society, the savoir-faire of businesspeople may help the organization to grow in the modern world and to communicate to a large audience a knowledge that had previously been restricted to a happy few.

As the circumstances have enabled me to be involved in Kyudo for so many years, I would like to contribute to its development in the years to come, and even after I have retired from my business responsibilities.

When you have a calling – whatever hobby it is – continue to follow it with sincerity and determination year after year. It might be a hidden treasure that will be revealed in the later part of your life.

Reception for the Kyudo World Cup, in the presence
of her Imperial Highness, Princess Takamado,
at the Embassy of France in Tokyo.

Shukusha shooting performed by Charles-Louis Oriou,
Jérôme Chouchan, and Claude Luzet (left to right).

IF YOU WANT TO IMPROVE YOUR BUSINESS, LOOK TO YOURSELF

19

Improving a business starts with seeing everything as your own responsibility.

FAILURE IS NOT BORN FROM OTHERS

In Kyudo, we say, "You make your own shots." This is a tautology because you are the one to shoot. But what this means is that you are responsible for building the form of your shooting with your own mind and body, much like a sculptor, who creates a statue from the wood available.

Of course, as you learn the way of Kyudo, Kyudo instructors offer advice, but you are the one who is responsible for making your own shots. Even if you ask desperately, no teacher can give you a formula that will solve all your shooting difficulties. No one else can shoot in your place.

In France, where I grew up, everything was a competition. We were taught to compete: the important thing was to win. This is not solely my experience: I think many young people are taught in this way and feel the same.

This was why maybe I decided to study so hard and went through a very selective examination to enter the French Grandes Ecoles HEC.

But when I encountered the teachings of Kyudo at the age of 29, it was totally different from the European style of thinking. While the world is about achieving outward results, Kyudo is first and foremost a battle fought only in the mind and body, against oneself. Kyudo has competitions, but you essentially compete against yourself. If you cannot shoot correctly, then you are the one who is responsible. You do not blame the results on anyone. If you fail, you do not search for external excuses. The Chinese classic, *The Book of Rites*, which is a core text of the Confucian canon says, "When the shooting falters, there is no resentment towards those who win. Instead, use the moment to search for yourself." The main focus of Kyudo training and practice is self-improvement. The *Book of Rites* was written more than 1,100 years ago, but it provides lessons on modern management. In recent leadership books, these simple forgotten truths have been rediscovered, and some authors advise that, in order to become an inspiring leader we must 'manage ourselves' or 'lead ourselves first'.

HABITS TO BUILD SUCCESS IN A COMPANY

When things do not go well in different situations, we tend to look for external excuses. In business, we may seek to blame competitors, our boss, the work environment, the market situation, the business climate, and so on and so forth.

In Kyudo, you build the contrary habit, which is to look into yourself first. You stop looking for the cause of failures in other people or situations. I believe this is one of the best things you can learn through Kyudo. It is also a trait you can practise in a company when you are in a managing position.

In practice, in the archery hall or in the workplace, this is difficult: it can be painful to be accountable for one's own shortcomings. But this is the only way to grow as a leader. Unfortunately, this is sometimes not the value of some individuals in positions of power and it is frequent to hear from top management that, "The strategy is right but the execution is wrong so we have to change the people." As top management is in charge of strategy, this is the way to put the blame on others.

Young people, also, encounter many unexpected events and obstacles as they enter the real world and experience new things. It is very easy to blame one's colleagues or the boss. But instead of blaming others, and then seeking to abandon past mistakes and work for another company, you should first re-examine yourself. If you build this habit, then your leadership skills will be seeded and flourish in due course.

In the past, Japanese companies used to take care of their employees like a parent, and the employees were able to gain better positions and better benefits, as long as they gained seniority in the organization. But with the fluctuations in the economy, and the spread of globalization, many Japanese companies have been forced to restructure their organizations, and the good old Japanese company system is becoming a thing of the past. In this context, it is increasingly important for Japanese employees to communicate what they want from the company in order to improve their skills and gain experience. It is also crucial for the company to listen to and answer these requests. In instances where learning and growing is no longer occurring, the employee needs to be ready to decide to leave the company or the department they are in.

In the archery hall, as in the workplace in Japan and around the world, it is imperative for everyone to be fully responsible and accountable for their own shooting.

EVERY SHOT IS YOUR LAST

20

If you fear adventure, life will never begin. Your encounters with people are your greatest treasure.

THE UNKNOWN COUNTRY, JAPAN

In the summer of 1983, I came to Japan for the first time after visiting the Philippines and Thailand. I was a college student then. Driven by my passion to see the unknown, I travelled through Southeast Asian countries, finally reaching Japan.

To drown in the abyss – heaven or hell,
Who cares? Through the unknown, we'll find the new.

Baudelaire, *Les Fleurs du Mal* [*Flowers of Evil*], 1857.

I have always loved literature; it filled me with curiosity. As a young man, I felt like the famous French poet Baudelaire. Of course, for someone like me, who was raised in Europe, visits to other Southeast Asian countries satisfied my curiosity for the exotic. But my purpose for visiting Japan was something more spiritual. I had a strong intuition that, in this far-Eastern country, there was something very different from European culture.

I had been charmed by the world of Zen and I had read a great deal about it. Zen was offering something totally different from the European way of thinking. The day after I came to Japan, I stood at the entrance to the Tomei Highway, holding up a paper that said 'Fukui'. I was going to Eihei-ji in Fukui. Eihei-ji is a temple famous for Zen training, founded by Dogen, who brought Soto Zen from China in the 13th century. It was eight o'clock at night and not easy to find a driver who was willing to pick up a foreign young man, hitchhiking at the entrance of the highway. At the moment when I had almost given up, thinking that hitchhiking would not work in Japan, a man in a camping car stopped for me. He was not going to Fukui, but gave me a ride to Gotemba, which was halfway to Fukui.

On the way to Gotemba, I learned that the man who stopped for me was Yoshimasa Sugawara, a living Japanese legend of the Dakar Rally. He had entered the Paris Dakar Rally for the first time in January of that year. Since he had just come back from France, he was very happy that he had happened to pick up a young French man, and he stopped at an 'onsen' (hot spring) and treated me to a sukiyaki dinner.

At the time, I did not know any Japanese, and spoke only English and French, yet we had a great conversation using a dictionary, and both had a very good time. We promised to meet again some time, and said good-bye. After that, hitchhiking went smoothly, and I was able to get to Eihei-ji. I applied for Zen training, but to my great surprise I found out that advance booking was required through a formal letter. I was told that even if I applied for it right then, the booking was full, and I would have to wait for some time. I had come all that way, but the door was closed, and I was clueless as to what to do. I was really in despair because I thought the world of Zen had escaped from me.

Anyway, I had no other choice to leave Eihei-ji and decided to hitchhike again. I had to find a place to stay. A kind man driving a small black van gave me a ride and, when I talked to him about what had happened at Eihei-ji, he introduced himself as the head priest of Tenryu-ji of Soto Zen, Kosen Sasagawa Roshi. My prior sentiment of despair immediately transformed itself into a burst of joy. He proposed that I stay at his temple. At Tenryu-ji, Reverend Sasagawa gave me Zazen training every morning and evening for a week, and then an intensive Zazen session for a couple of days called 'sesshin', literally 'touching the heart-mind'. He told me that he would talk to Eihei-ji so that I could practice there also. So, thanks to the help of those who I met in Japan, I was able to achieve my goal of receiving zen training at Eihei-ji.

After that, I travelled around Hokuriku prefecture, before returning to Tokyo and meeting Sugawara again. He invited me to stay at his house the night before I went back to France.

Many years later, when I discussed with Sugawara about my luck to have been able at that time to practise at Eiheiji, he told me a Japanese proverb: "When you want something very strongly, the way to get it opens up." This reminded me of "Seek and you will find" (*Matthew*, 7:7).

TO JAPAN ONCE MORE

Back in France, my memory of my summer spent in Japan had begun to fade by autumn. That is when I learned that a magazine for students in France, *l'Etudiant*, was calling for entries in a competition in writing a paper on a plan to do PR for Japanese culture. *l'Etudiant* was a very famous magazine that every college student in France knew about. The theme given for the paper was Japanese culture, which I had just experienced. It felt as if it was given just for me. I knew right away what I could write about. I would describe the scenery of training at Eihei-ji and the questions I had.

The title of my paper was, "Why do big corporations in Japan send their new recruits to Zen temples for training?"

Young graduates spend a short period of time at a temple for training and get refreshed, and to prepare to enter the new world of corporate Japan. To me, this seemed very peculiar, because in Europe we did not have a significant gap between college life and working life.

The aim of my intended study, as outlined in my paper was for me – the planner – to go to a Zen temple for training in order to discover the reason behind this cultural tradition, and then write a report on it. It was a very appealing project. If I won the competition, I could return to Japan. So, I wrote about my experience in Japan and entered it into the competition. I was confident about the contents of the paper, but I was not sure if I was able to communicate well enough for the judges to find it interesting. In January of the following year, I received a surprising notice. My paper had won first place, which gave me an opportunity to go back to Japan as a prize.

THE MYSTERY OF THE WORD 'EN'

When I look back on these days, I can see how valuable it was for me to meet Sugawara and Reverend Sasagawa. At that time, I could not speak Japanese and did not know anything about Japanese culture. They helped me and afforded me an opportunity.

Now I describe these events as being an 'en'. When I look up the word 'en' in an English dictionary, it says 'karma, destiny, fate, chance, relation'. However, having lived in Japan for a long time, I discovered that the word 'en', is used a great deal in everyday life, for various occasions, ranging from meeting a new person to finding a new job, or even buying a new product that you like… You meet someone and something happens. And then your relationship with that person has started and it bears fruit. In hindsight, the encounter was, you could say, already there in a latent invisible form, just waiting for the occasion to manifest itself in real life.

The mystery of en is that it is not planned or predicted; it just happens out of the blue. As with hitchhiking, there is no guarantee that a car will stop for you, or that anyone would pick you up and drive you somewhere. In this type of situation, en happens when you open up your heart.

In business, you will start meeting many people when you believe in the power of en, which leads to many unexpected and wonderful things. The most fruitful relationships in my life were born from chance encounters, encounters through en – not through social connections, formal introductions, or plans. My interactions with people then led me to places I never expected to be.

Had I not met Sugawara at the highway entrance that day, I might not have made it to Fukui. If I had not met Rev. Sasagawa who picked up a hitchhiker like me, I might not have received any training at Eihei-ji. If I had not received any training at Eihei-ji, I would not have written that paper, and I may not have visited Japan again. My first trip to Japan would have ended as a pleasant memory from my youth.

And now, I am working with Godiva Japan as an extension of a series of those encounters. This precious experience taught me the following: that actions breed encounters; encounters breed opportunities for success. Unless you take action, nothing will happen.

I do not hitchhike at the entrance of a highway any longer. Hitchhiking was a meaningful action to a young man in his twenties. But I still 'hitchhike' in a way that is appropriate for me right now. I meet people – not just through plans and set-ups – but by chance, and I enjoy every instant of those encounters: each moment happens only once in a lifetime. Actions breed new encounters, and these meetings make my life fruitful. I will continue to hitchhike through life, seeking valuable experiences that touch our hearts. Life embraced in this way becomes richer, fuller and more rewarding.

Note:

Yoshimasa Sugawara, who picked me up while hitchhiking, has continued to enter the Paris Dakar Rally since 1983; he achieved 32 consecutive entries in 2015. Including the 2008 rally, which was called off, he has made 33 consecutive entries. This is an unprecedented record and was listed in the Guinness World Records in 2008.

Reverend Kosen Sasagawa is still a resident priest of Tenryu-ji and is popular among people as Sage Sasagawa.

EVERY SHOT IS YOUR LAST

There is an important saying in Kyudo: "Every shot is your last" (issha zetsumei). Literally, 'isha' means 'one shot' and 'zetsumei' means 'end of life.' Thus, when you enter the archery hall for your shooting – when you move to the shooting place, and start your movement for your shooting, until the arrow is released – you should have the firm intent to do your very best, as if after the very act of this shooting, you will die. The bow was an instrument of war in the battlefield, so the thought of life and death was always there in the minds of the archers. Now, in peace time, as we said earlier, the enemy is no more outside the archer but *inside*. Japanese archery has evolved into a fight against oneself (jibun to no tatakai) as a Way to self-development. Practicing Issha Zetsumei in archery and daily life means that you realize that this moment is a treasure, and you should do your best at this very instant.

The Persian Sufi Rumi expressed the same discipline, in a verse of *Matwani* (1-132-3): "The Sufi is the son of the Moment. It is not the rule of the Way to say 'tomorrow'."

Life is a series of irreplaceable moments. Each moment is a moment that only you own. By grasping the teaching of Kyudo, whether you practice it in the archery hall or implement its principles in the work place, you can polish your character, grow, and hit your targets. Both at work and life you must make decisions, take actions, reflect on the results, and then act again. Shot after shot, by seizing each moment, you will build the shining form of your life.

In the Shiseikan Dojo in Tokyo, these two ideograms are written on
the curtain of the target bank: sincerity (makoto) and reach (itaru).
This encourages the archer, while aiming at the target,
to express utmost sincerity through his shooting.

LOOKING FORWARD

In search of noble purpose and personal fulfilment. The company of the future will blend the techniques of management with discipline of the mind.

In business as in archery, there is only one result: we either hit or miss the target. In Kyudo, right shooting always results in a hit. In business, proper management always results in sustainable and profitable growth.

The essential questions are why and how we face the target.

The entrepreneur and the senior executive is the hero of our modern age. In the myths of ancient Greece, Hercules faced a crossroad with two paths: the left path was called Vice, the right path named Virtue. This is not an easy or simple choice. The path of vice is to follow the desire of the self. The path of virtue involves striving for something greater than oneself. Each path has its own obstacles, dynamics and fruits along the way.

In business, there will be always two paths to reach the target: financial performance as the sole measure of everything, or financial performance as a result of doing first and foremost the right thing for the consumer, the employee and society as a whole.

In the future, the meaning and purpose of work is bound to change dramatically. In developed countries, voices from young generations are already demanding more meaning and happiness in the workplace. In time, there will be a tipping point, where the present values of what we call 'work' or 'a job' will be transformed and a new order will emerge. The job will not be a means to an end, but will be a 'praxis' in the Aristotelian sense of "bringing joy by the operation itself". The job will offer an opportunity to satisfy the essential needs of the human being: spiritual, psychological and physical, according to the three constituting elements of man: spirit, soul and body.

In the meantime, we are still in a period of transition and in most companies an unengaged workforce is still the norm.

However, we do not need to be pessimistic. Every one of us can contribute in our own way to building a better workplace. For those who are on a path of self-development, as we have seen with Kyudo, every obstacle should be seen as material to work upon: an opportunity to perfect the character and grow.

In feudal Japan, the Way of the Samurai was called 'Bun Bu Ryo Do': The Way of Culture and Martial Arts. Both studies of liberal and martial arts were prerequisites to becoming a respected leader. In the modern area, where business has become the driving force of society, Peter Drucker anticipated that management should be a liberal art, dealing with wisdom and practice.

I believe that the businessperson who performs every day in a company can get inspiration from ancient wisdoms and arts. We have shown the example of Kyudo, from Japan. Kyudo taught us that practice of technique alone is not enough, and that discipline of the mind is necessary to bring the technique to life. Similarly, business is not solely about the techniques of management, but also about the man who performs the task. The strategies of management are changing rapidly with the times, but the soul of man is the same as it was a few thousand years ago. In a fast-moving, globalized world, inspiration from ancient wisdoms and arts has relevance to business now more than ever. This is a journey that each of us can embark upon with sincerity and determination. Progress along the Way will improve the man, the company and society as a whole.

BIBLIOGRAPHY

All Nippon Kyudo Federation, *Kyudo Manual*, 1994.

Aristotle, *Nichomachean Ethics*,
Cambridge University Press, 2014.

Baudelaire Charles, *The Flowers of Evil*,
Oxford University Press, 2008.

Coomaraswammy, Ananda K., *The Transformation of Nature in Art*, Munshiram Manoharlal Publishers Pvt.Ltd, 1994.

Coomaraswamy, Ananda K., *Christian and Oriental Philosophy of Art*, Dover Publications, 2011.

Christensen Clayton M., *Competing Against Luck*,
HarperBusiness, 2016.

Confucius, *The Book of Rites*, CreateSpace Independent Publishing Platform, 2013.

Confucius, *Confucius Analects*, translated by Edward
Slingerland, Hackett Publishing Company, Inc, 2003.

Druker, Peter, *Management: Tasks, Responsibilities, Practices*,
HarperBusiness, 1993.

Guenon Rene, *The Reign of Quantity & The Signs of
The Times*, Sophia Perennis, 2004.

Herrigel, Eugen, *Zen in the Art of Archery*,
Vintage Books Edition, 1989.

Onuma Hideharu with Dan and Jackie DeProspero,
Kyudo: The Essence and Practice of Japanese Archery,
Kodansha International Ltd, 1993.

Lao tse, *Tao Te King* (French edition), translated by
J-J-L Duyvendak, J. Maisonneuve, 1987.

Legge James (translator), *The I-Ching or The Book of Changes*, CreateSpace Independent Publishing Platform, 2008.

Nitobe Inazo, *Bushido: The Soul of Japan*, Kodansha International, 2012.

Rumi, Mawlana Jalal-ad-Din Muhammad, *The Masnavi I Ma'navi of Rumi*, CreateSpace Independent Publishing Platform, 2011.

Takuan Soho, *Fudochi Shin Myoroku: The Mysterious Record of Immovable Wisdom*, CreateSpace Independent Publishing Platform, 2016.

Winthrop Sargeant (translator), *Bhagavad Gita*, State University of New York Press, 1994.

ABOUT THE
AUTHOR

Jérôme Chouchan is the Managing Director of Godiva Chocolatier for Japan, South Korea, the rest of Asia (except Greater China), Australia and New Zealand. He has extensive management experience in Japan and Asia, having worked for premium global brands such as Lacoste, Hennessy and Lladro. He has a master's degree in management from the Grande Ecole HEC Paris.

Jérôme Chouchan has practiced Kyudo in Japan for more than 25 years and holds a Kyudo Renshi (instructor license) and a 5th dan degree. He is also a Board Director of the Kyudo International Federation, the body governing the development of Kyudo globally.

He published *Target* in Japanese in 2016.

25TH LID ANNIVERSARY

Sharing knowledge since 1993

- 1993 Madrid
- 2008 Mexico DF and Monterrey
- 2010 London
- 2011 New York and Buenos Aires
- 2012 Bogotá
- 2014 Shanghai and San Francisco